THE LONDON BUS GUIDE

The Routes ~ The Buses
The Garages ~ The Companies

CONTENTS

Foreword

The London bus scene isn't just about tourist sights in central London. The area covered by TfL is vast, and there are plenty of rural spots like this one to contrast with the congestion of the city. A Dennis Dart with a Marshall Capital body approaches Orpington High Street.

The purpose of this guide is to explain the operation of Transport for London's (TfL) bus routes and to make your visit to the Capital more rewarding and enjoyable. The book is designed to be taken out and used as a quick reference guide when you visit the London area, so the information is presented in a way we would have found useful when visiting locations for the first time. With this in mind, your feedback will be welcomed so we can modify and improve future editions.

There is one proviso: Because of the nature of London bus operations (and despite our best efforts to provide an accurate picture), you need to be aware that *the scene is constantly changing.* What you see today may be completely different tomorrow (and *vice versa*). The information is correct to 17th September 2011 and we have also highlighted future changes, where known, on the opening page of the relevant section. However, no

book can hope to give you every quirky little detail. You need to get out and explore for yourself. We hope this book provides a significant nudge in the right direction.

I must also thank the following:

Alan Millar, Editor of *Buses* magazine, for his useful advice, and for busting a few myths about the London bus world. David Maxey, for re-writing the text and captions and supplying some of the detailed information. The photograhers who've plugged the gaps in our photo collection, and the garage staff who've patiently answered our endless questions this year.

I hope you find this book useful in your exploration of London.

Ken Carr
Boreham, Essex,
September 2011

London Bus Network Overview

The London network is unique in Britain in that it's the only one to be regulated. The buses are organised by TfL's subsidiary London Bus Services Ltd, trading as London Buses (LB). It is this body that decides which routes are run and the service levels to be operated. LB also monitors service quality and is responsible for bus stations, bus stops, fares, revenue protection, radio and vehicle tracking equipment, roadside staff to deal with diversions and major incidents, and the marketing of the London network.

More than 700 routes are operated and more than 100 of those are 24-hour, 7 days a week. In addition, 600-series routes provide morning and afternoon school journeys in term time, and a declining number of mobility services (900-series routes) operate once a week.

Since the year 2000, there has been a dramatic increase in London bus usage. Mileage is up 32%, ridership approximately 70% - staggering growth figures by any standard.

Contracts

Bus services within the TfL area are operated by private companies under contract to London Buses. Contracts are awarded route by route, normally for a period of five years. However, under the Quality Incentive (QI) scheme, there is an option to extend each route's contract by two years. As the name suggests, the aim is to incentivise operators to provide quality service during the core contract period. Although routes are generally tendered individually, others in the same area often come up for renewal at the same time to make changeovers easier.

The tendering programme is continuous, with between 15% and 20% of the network typically offered each year. Tender evaluation focuses on best value for money, but also takes into account safety and quality as essential features. Contract payments are directly linked to the mileage each route runs and to the overall reliability of the service. Comprehensive quality measurements are in place across all aspects of delivery.

Before offering a tender, London Buses reviews each route to produce a service specification detailing the route that buses will take (including terminal arrangements), service frequency at different times of day and on different days of the week (including the times of first and last buses), and the type and capacity of vehicle to be used. Operators are then asked to provide a schedule for delivering the specified level of service, along with the base cost of meeting this level plus a profit margin.

Although London Buses operates an approved supplier list, it routinely places advertisements in the Official Journal of the European Union seeking expressions of interest from potential operators. Once a new applicant has been assessed and approved, it is then able to compete in the route-by-route tendering process. Invitations to Tender (ITTs) are issued every 2-4 weeks.

Route sizes vary considerably, as does each route's Peak Vehicle Requirement (PVR). This is the number of buses required to operate the service at times of greatest frequency - usually the morning and evening 'rush hours', but not exclusively so - and it ranges from one to more than fifty. Services are classified as either High Frequency (5 buses or more per hour throughout much of the week) or Low Frequency (4 buses per hour or fewer). About 82% of the network is High Frequency. The highest frequency routes have a bus every 2-3 minutes, the lowest frequency routes have only a single return journey each day. Most routes operate from about 04.30 am till midnight, but an increasing number run 24 hours a day. Some routes 'morph' into night bus services between midnight and 04.30 (87 becomes N87, for example) with their daytime routes extended or modified.

Within the tender documentation, London Buses also specifies the minimum requirements for the vehicles to be used. The operator may choose the vehicle manufacturer, so long as its vehicles meet the criteria in the specification (like potential operators, new bus models are individually assessed and approved by TfL). Tenders are submitted on a sealed bid basis and must contain all relevant information for London Buses to make an effective evaluation.

The award of Contracts is based on achieving the most economically advantageous outcome within the resources available. The criteria include:

Price Ability - to deliver quality services to the levels specified in the ITT.

Staffing Ability - to recruit, train and retain personnel of a suitable calibre.

Premises - the suitability of an existing depot, and/or the operator's ability to obtain a suitable depot.

Vehicles - the type proposed and any additional features they offer above the tender specification. The operator's ability to maintain vehicles in an acceptable condition throughout the life of the contract is a major consideration.

Financial Status - the operator's resources to fund start-up costs and provide stability over the contract term.

Schedules - compliance with the specifications.

Tender evaluation is led by a Contracts Tendering Manager supported by a small team of skilled

technical and commercial staff. Recommendations for contract awards are discussed and approved by the Tender Evaluation Committee, comprising the directors of London Bus Services Ltd.

As mentioned above, there is a nominated gross cost attached to each contract (operating costs plus profit), but the Quality Incentive aspect also provides for performance bonuses and/or deductions, as well as the two-year extension option. Each contract also has a specified Minimum Performance Standard reflecting the particular characteristics of the route. Performance monitoring data obtained by London Buses is normally shared with the operator. The contract price is adjusted each year in line with inflation.

The Quality Incentive scheme and performance monitoring are inextricably linked, covering not only service reliability but also driving quality and vehicle condition. The latter two are monitored by a combination of 'mystery traveller' surveys and vehicle inspections at garages. All of this is combined in a set of 'extension threshold' criteria in the tender documentation which, if met, trigger the automatic two-year extension. The operator can choose to decline, in which case the route would be re-tendered immediately at the end of the contract. In the event of acceptance, the extension is on the same basis as the original contract and the route is removed from the tendering renewal process for two years.

Although operators are expected to deliver the full contracted service, this is not always possible. Mechanical breakdowns, staff sickness, roadworks, road closures and other incidents on or near the route can all have a negative effect, hence the minimum performance standard. Any mileage which cannot be operated is split into two categories: Deductible Lost Mileage (loss of route operation considered to be within the Operator's reasonable control, e.g. staff absence, mechanical breakdown) and Non-Deductible Lost Mileage (instances beyond the Operator's reasonable control, such as adverse traffic conditions). Obviously, the Operator is not paid for Deductible Lost Mileage, and the deduction is calculated on a pro rata basis.

London's environmental issues and poor air quality have been rapidly climbing the list of priorities for tender assessment in recent years. New vehicles have to conform to the latest European emissions standards, and operators are also encouraged to introduce higher standards sooner than European law requires. Buses operating on the London network have a minimum standard of Euro-2 until 3rd January 2012 when Euro-4 becomes the minimum. The most recent standard is Euro-5, and each of these progressive steps relates (in the main) to the effectiveness of the vehicles' diesel particulate filters.

With pollution in mind (and the constant threat of heavy fines being imposed by the EU), Transport

TfL has opted for diesel-electric hybrid buses as one solution to London's pollution problem. However, the hybrids accounted for only 106 deliveries between 2006 and 2010 - a drop in the ocean considering the size of the London fleet. Metroline operates fifteen Enviro400 hybrids on Routes 16 & 139, with another 26 on order.

for London is trialling the latest advances in vehicle technology, including a batch of hydrogen fuel cell buses which produce no polluting emissions. Diesel-electric hybrids (powered by smaller engines and batteries charged by regenerative braking) also produce lower emissions than a traditional diesel bus. Various designs are in service with six different operators, but mass introduction seems distant as the 106 vehicles put onto the streets in the past five years have all been subsidised by the government's Green Fund. However, a further 96 of varying kinds are due for delivery in the second half of 2011 and it has recently been announced that Go-Ahead will be bucking the trend by meeting the extra costs itself for the Route 19 conversion, due in March 2012 and involving 15 hybrid buses. So, London-wide, only 8,000 to go.

Other Services

London Buses also procures buses for rail replacement journeys on behalf of London Underground. More than 100 such contracts are issued in advance of planned engineering work each year. Some involve only a single bus, others

can require fifty. The tendering process is similar to that used for normal services and front-line operators such as First Group and Abellio regularly win these contracts. Smaller companies currently without TfL routes, such as Ensign and Sullivan Buses, can also appear on this work.

London Buses' Dial-a-Ride service is run for the benefit of disabled and elderly people. The service initially used a fleet of Mercedes-Benz minibuses, but these are rapidly being replaced by a fleet of Bluebird Tuscanas painted in the familiar TfL Red and owned by London Buses itself. Booking one is similar to booking a taxi, although the passenger has to pre-register before being able to use the service. He or she can then phone a call centre with details of the journey they wish to make and they're given a pick-up time, varying 15 minutes either way. However, they may have to share a vehicle with other passengers on a journey likely to involve pick-ups & set-downs for others. For this reason, there is no guarantee the route will be direct, but the service is free and a commendable addition to London Buses' operations. The Go-Ahead company in London runs a Commercial Services Fleet, with a variety of older

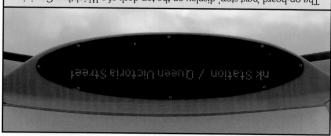

nk Station / Queen Victoria Street

The on-board 'next stop' display on the top deck of a Wrightbus Gemini.

bus types including the much-loved Routemaster. These buses are available for general hire and also appear on special services linked to some of London's big annual events like the Chelsea Flower Show and the Wimbledon Tennis Championships. Regular members of the fleet, identifiable by their gold numbers, are augmented at busy times by their vehicles of similar type (like the PVL class) normally engaged on TfL contracts.

iBus!

Every bus operating a TfL route is fitted with the Automatic Vehicle Location (AVL) system, better known as iBus. It works using a combination of technologies, including the Global Positioning System (GPS) and 'map matching', which

receives input from a gyroscope and the bus's speedometer/odometer.

The bus data radio uses GPS to send its location to a central computer system approximately every 30 seconds. This information is available to service controllers monitoring performance along the route and enables them to take action to improve service reliability. It is not uncommon to hear drivers receiving radio messages from controllers instructing them to wait time in at a stop to reduce the 'bunching' that can occur when traffic conditions are bad. As well as the driver-generated adjustments, TfL can also send instructions directly to traffic lights, altering the timing of their phases to help speed up buses when congestion occurs.

The bus's on-board computer carries the details of every stop along the route and all of the possible destinations. The computer constantly tracks the bus's position from the AVL. The computer information and announces each stop as it occurs, using pre-recorded 'sound bites'. Digital displays on both decks convey the same information to the hearing-impaired. Important locations close

The London Dial-a-Ride service is upgrading from Mercedes-Benz mini-buses to Volkswagen T5 Bluebird Tuscanas. These are 6.8 metre vehicles licensed to carry eight passengers. One of the first to be introduced in 2008, D7003, pauses at the chip shop in Kingsbury.

Countdown screens fitted to an increasing number of bus shelters provide 'next bus due' information for all routes serving the stop.

and deducts the fare from the credit balance on the card. The process repeats for subsequent journeys until the daily cap (currently £4.00 for buses only across all zones) is reached.

Children aged under 11 travel free; 11 to 15s travel free if they have an 11-15 Oyster photocard. Further concessions apply to those aged 16 to 18. Over-60s resident in London can apply for a Freedom Pass allowing free off-peak travel on buses and the rail network. A similar scheme is available to the disabled. Most over-60s living outside of London can apply for an English bus pass from their local authority. Since 2008, these passes have been

to stops, such as hospitals, are also announced visually and aurally.

Centre Comm - London Buses' 24/7 Emergency Command and Control Centre - can also use the bus PA system to communicate directly with passengers in the event of an emergency. Similarly, the driver can make contact with Centre Comm if an accident occurs, allowing the incident to be pin-pointed precisely when emergency assistance is despatched.

The central computer system also predicts the time it will take for buses to arrive at stops. Each bus's arrival can then be displayed on LED countdown indicators at key bus shelters. This 'real time' system is now installed at more than 2,000 locations. The next development will be the potential for passengers to check bus information in real time on their smart-phones.

As a continual process, iBus also provides detailed journey data which operators can use to improve individual routes.

Ticketing

All fares revenue goes directly to TfL and fares are collected in a number of ways. London buses accept Travelcards, Oyster Card products, bus passes and single journey cash fares. The latter used to be charged on length of journey (based on fare stages), but there is now only one flat fare. From 2000, this became higher for journeys in Zone 1 than in outer zones, but the difference was eliminated in 2004 with the introduction of Oyster Card flat fares. Cash fares are considerably higher than Oyster fares for the same journey.

With the Oyster Card 'pay as you go' (formerly Pre-Pay), users are charged a fixed amount for single journeys, but a 'daily cap' limits the maximum deducted from the balance on a card, regardless of how many buses are used that day (a day is measured from 4.30 am to 4.30 am). Weekly and monthly passes can also be purchased and loaded onto an Oyster Card. On boarding the bus, the Oyster Card is held up to a 'reader' which registers the journey

To speed up loading times, passengers must obtain valid tickets in advance for all bendybus routes and within the central London 'cashless zone'. Single journey tickets, for those without Oyster cards or other passes, can be bought from pavement machines.

Throughout the year enthusiast groups organise road runs with preserved buses on former routes they once served. RML902 arrives at North Weald Bus Rally after a Route 104 run.

accepted England-wide and provide free travel on all TfL routes after 9.30 am on weekdays and any time at weekends. *[Please note: If you are approaching your 60th birthday and plan to apply for one of these concessions, the age qualification is gradually being raised from 60 to 65 to save money. However, you are eligible immediately if you were born before 6th April 1950. There are similar schemes for residents of Scotland and Wales, but these passes are not accepted on TfL routes.]*

Cash customers travelling on the remaining bendibuses and on Route W7 must buy tickets before boarding from the bus stop ticket machines. The route numbers this requirement applies to are marked in yellow on bus stop displays along with 'Buy tickets before boarding'. Drivers on these routes do not issue tickets and there are Oyster 'repeaters' in the centre of bendibuses for passengers boarding through the middle and rear doors.

Additionally, many bus stops within the West End of London fall within a 'cashless area' designed to speed up the boarding process. Here,

too, passengers must have a valid ticket or pass before boarding. Outside the cashless area, single tickets (£2.20 as of Sept 2011) may be bought from the bus driver.

For the Enthusiast . . .

London has lots to offer (lots of buses for one thing) and there are a number of 'hot spot' locations where you can enjoy a wide variety of types. If you

Trade stands set up alongside vintage vehicles at a Potters Bar garage open day.

have never been to central London before, the area between Trafalgar Square and Aldwych is especially recommended. At the latter location, for instance, you can see (on a good day) hydrogen fuel cell buses running alongside heritage Routemasters and many of the standard Alexander Dennis and Wrightbus models. Please refer to the 'Buses' section of this book for what can be found where.

During the year, various organisations have 'road runs' featuring a variety of older buses retracing routes they served in the dim and distant past. It's also worth keeping an eye out for garage open-days. Metroline's Potters Bar garage open day in July is becoming an annual event. As well as the garage's regular types, a host of heritage buses visit and you can take free rides on them around the local area. Metroline usually holds a second open day during the year. In 2011 it's at Holloway in north London on 1st October.

To enhance your London experience, we recommend the various bus route maps. TfL produces a set of five free maps - a central London version and the rest of the area split into four quadrants - north-east, south-west, et cetera. These are also very useful for tracing Overground and Underground railways through the London area. The TfL maps are available from larger Tube stations and Travel Information Centres like the one at Victoria main line station. They can also be downloaded from the web in PDF format. Go to: www.tfl.gov.uk/tfl/getting around/maps/buses/bus diagrams.asp and scroll to the bottom of the page.

Alternatively, you can buy a map, especially the one many enthusiasts swear by - Mike Harris's Greater London Bus Map for around £2.00. A Night Bus version is also available. Further information from: www.busmap.co.uk

Further Reading

The London Omnibus Traction Society (LOTS) publishes an annual pocket-size fleet book listing the running numbers and registrations of each bus, operator by operator. The 2011 version costs £6.95. Go to: www.lots.org.uk

British Bus Publishing publishes a London Bus Handbook. This A5 production is much heavier and glossier and includes garage allocations for each bus as well as plenty of colour photos. It retails at £18.25. See www.britishbuspublishing.co.uk for further information.

LOTS is the main enthusiast society in the London area, which it covers in considerable detail in its monthly magazine The London Bus. This is available direct to your home in return for an annual membership fee of £22.00, or you can buy

individual copies at places like the Ian Allan shops.

Further details from: LOTS, Unit N305, Westminster Business Square, 1-45 Durham Street, Vauxhall, London SE11 5JH or via the website: www.lots.org.uk

The PSV Circle reports monthly on the London bus scene via news sheets. A year's-worth costs £19.00 and you can start by visiting: www.psv-circle.org.uk

The Omnibus Society has a London Historical Research Group. Full details of this can be found at: www.Omnibussoc.org

While we're on the web, there are two other sites which are truly excellent.

The first - www.londonbusroutes.net - is a useful resource for the most recent/forthcoming changes.

The second - www.londonbusesbyadam.zenfolio.com - is a photo site with more than 13,000 images featuring every route in London.

The Operators

Although comparative calm has descended since the organised chaos provoked by bus deregulation, changes continue to occur from time to time in 'who operates what' in London. The biggest operators are Arriva and Go-Ahead, each with more than 20% of the total peak vehicle requirement. The smallest are CT Plus and Quality Line, both with less than 1%. Here is some potted history of the main companies, which also reveals the extent of worldwide financial interest in running London's buses.

Abellio is ultimately owned by the Nederlandse Spoorwegen of Holland, originally through its subsidiary NedRailways. In May 2009 the company bought Travel London (and the smaller Travel Surrey) from the National Express Group. Travel London came into being when NatEx bought the French-owned Connex Bus in 2004. A year later it bought Tellings-Golden Miller as well. After the most recent sale, the Travel London designation would have been retained but for NedRailways changing its name to Abellio Group in October 2009.

Arriva's first venture into London can be traced back to 1980 when the company was still known as Cowie, after the family who started the company in Sunderland in the 1930s. Cowie bought Grey-Green - basically a fast commuter coach service provider - in 1980. Seven years later, Grey-Green

successfully tendered for some London routes. In 1994 the Cowie Group bought Leaside Buses, then the last LBL subsidiary, South London Transport. The group changed its name to Arriva in 1997. Further acquisitions followed - Kentish Bus in 1997, County Bus in 1998 and Londonlinks in 1999. Arriva has the distinction of having been the first to operate the bendibus in London and the last to operate Routemasters in normal daily service (as opposed to heritage). You may have noticed from other London bus publications that Arriva the Shires and Arriva Southern Counties Group (and their bus fleets) are listed separately from Arriva London. This is because they are separate companies operating from different Head Offices. Our book follows that convention.

First Group began operating London buses in 1997 when it acquired Centrewest. This was later followed by Capital Citybus, a former Hong Kong-based business bought out by local management, in 1998. Both of these, and operations in north London, now come under the First London banner.

Go-Ahead London is the collective name of the Go-Ahead Group's various operations in the capital. Based in Newcastle, its first London venture was the acquisition of London Buses Ltd. subsidiary London Central in September 1994. Another former LBL subsidiary, London General, which had initially

A front end contrast from different decades outside St Paul's Underground station: Stagecoach ALX400 19229 draws up beside HV8, an Arriva B5L/Gemini hybrid.

been a management buy-out, was added in May 1996. The development of both companies since than has been on parallel lines, but a shred of distinctiveness between them remains.

Metrobus was added to the London operation in September 1999. Formed in 1983 from the wreckage of the Orpington & District bus company collapse, Metrobus has retained a separate identity - so much so, that it is hard to discern any physical connection between Stockwell buses (London General) and Orpington buses apart from their (mostly) red colour. Go-Ahead expanded its London operation further in September 2006 when London General bought Docklands Buses. Eight months later, the group acquired the contracted bus operations of Blue Triangle, but BT's MD, Roger Wright, understandably retained ownership of the heritage fleet. To complete the present shape of Go-Ahead London, the East Thames Buses brand was added in 2009 following a tendering process conducted by TfL.

The Go-Ahead London logo can be traced back to August 2008, although recent bus repaints have appeared with individual London General and London Central fleetnames beneath. There is also the vexed question of Go-Ahead's livery style, which somehow manages to dodge the 'buses must be red all over' edict issued by TfL.

London United was another LBL subsidiary subject to a management buy-out in 1994. Three years later, the French company Transdev bought it.

Sovereign London was acquired in 2002 (re-named London Sovereign from 2004) via the convoluted route of Borehamwood Travel Services (original company name), Blazefield (whose Sovereign subsidiary bought BTS in 1994, whereupon the London tag was added) and Transdev, which bought the whole of Blazefield in 2006. In 2009 the Transdev Group began negotiations with Veolia Environnement with the aim of merging itself with Veolia Transport. In the resulting agreement, made in May 2010, it was agreed that the RATP Group, which had a minority shareholding in Transdev, would assume ownership of some of Transdev's routes and assets in lieu of cash payment. This had a considerable impact on Transdev's London operations, splitting the company into two unequal parts.

London Sovereign's two garages and their routes remained with Transdev as part of the merged Veolia Transdev group, RATP got everything else, i.e. the eight garages of what was originally London United. The agreement took effect in March 2011, and the London United name re-emerged alongside much-reduced RATP Group branding. The small number of buses operating London Sovereign routes still defiantly proclaim themselves to be Transdev.

Metroline is another of the LBL companies from 1989, but acquired by the ComfortDelgro Group of Singapore in 2000. By then, Metroline had absorbed Atlas Bus (just after privatisation in 1994) London

Camberwell-based President PVL136 circumnavigates Aldgate while on a driver training run. This is one of the early batch (PVL1-143) with centre staircase.

TfL has decreed that London buses shall henceforth be 'red all over', apart from subtle fleet names and the compulsory roundel. First Group's recently-delivered Eclipse Gemini, VN36136, shows off the 'new look' at the Tower of London while deputising for a failed hydrogen bus on RV1.

Northern and R&I Buses in 1998. ComfortDelgro has added Thorpes (2004) and Armchair (2005).

The **Stagecoach** Company's interest in London began in 1994 when it bought LB's East London Bus & Coach Company and the South East London & Kent Bus Company (known as Selkent). Stagecoach pulled out of London in 2006, surprisingly, when it sold its entire operation to the Australian Macquarie Bank for £263 million. The new owners reintroduced the East London and Selkent fleetnames and in 2009 created Thameside for its Rainham-based buses. In an equally surprising move, Stagecoach re-acquired the whole lot in October 2010 for only £59 million, whereupon Stagecoach branding was rapidly reinstated.

Hackney Community Transport was established in 1982 when 30 community groups in the London Borough of Hackney formed a pool of six vehicles with a grant from Hackney Borough Council, aimed at providing low cost van and minibus hire for those groups and a door-to-door alternative to public transport for the disabled. HCT gained its first TfL contract in 2001 to operate route 153 under the CT Plus brand. Further contracts followed in 2003. In July 2006 HCT merged with Lambeth and Southwark Community Transport, and in 2008 began running a bendibus service to and from the Olympics 2012 site for construction workers.

Epsom Coaches made a move into the bus market in the 1980s de-regulation, and in 1997 expanded into London routes. The bus operation was re-branded as Quality Line in 2003 and, since then, has gradually gained new contracts.

Sullivan Buses will enter the fray in February 2012 after winning the contract for route 298. The company was formed in 1999 and currently runs routes in Hertfordshire, as well as rail replacement services for TfL, and a number of school journeys.

Ensignbus also runs rail replacements contracts. Until 1990, the company had some London routes but sold them to Citybus. After a brief return, this came to an end again in 1999.

A brief word about 'livery', if that's the right word anymore. As mentioned in the Go-Ahead paragraph, operators running TfL-contracted routes must now paint their buses all-red, apart from modest fleet names. So, the distinctive blue skirts on the Metroline buses are gradually disappearing, as will the grey/yellow stripes on Go-Ahead's fleet, the 'grey sandwich' of Transdev, Arriva's white horns, and the swirls of First Group. The white London bus roundel is appearing on the all-over red buses. Apart from that, the only other embellishment is the word 'Hybrid' in green on the latest diesel-electrics, replacing the shower of green leaves on the earlier examples and the claim that they were all the Mayor of London's doing.

Abellio

Garages

QB	Battersea
BC	Beddington
BF	Byfleet
TF	Fulwell
WS	Hayes
WL	Walworth

Fleet Total

619

Double Deckers - 303
Single Deckers - 316

PVR = 452

Head Office:
301 Camberwell New Road,
London, SE5 0TF

ROUTES OPERATED

3	35	40	100	112	117	152	156
157	172	188	211	235	322	343	344
350	381	407	414	434	452	481	484
490	931	941	969	C3	C10	H20	H25
H26	H28	N3	N35	N343	N381	P13	R68
R70	U7						

Single Deckers Operated

Dart - Nimbus
Dart - Pointer
Dart - Pointer 2
Dart - Spryte
E200Dart - Enviro200
Super Dart - East Lancs
Electrocity
Optare Solo

Double Deckers Operated

B7TL - Eclipse Gemini
Enviro400
Trident - ALX400

Abellio's double-deck fleet comprises three types, although hybrid Enviro400s are on order. ALX400 9836 stops at the east end of the Strand before heading south across Waterloo Bridge.

Arriva

Garages

AE	Ash Grove
DX	Barking
CN	Beddington
BN	Bixton
CT	Clapton
TC	Croydon
DT	Dartford
EC	Edmonton
E	Enfield
LV	Leeside Road
N	Norwood
AD	Palmers Green
SF	Stamford Hill
AR	Tottenham
TH	Thornton Heath
GR	Watford
WN	Wood Green

Fleet Total

1815

Double Deckers - 1401
Single Deckers - 414

PVR = 1423

Head Offices:

North: 16 Watsons Road, Wood Green N22 7TZ

South: Bus Garage, Brighton Road, Croydon CR2 6EL

Mercedes Citaro Gs waved goodbye to route 73 on 3rd September 2011, replaced by a mix of straight diesel and diesel-electric Wrightbus double-deckers. Arriva, which retained the route on changeover, has sent a large number of its discarded 'bendys' to work in Malta.

ROUTES OPERATED

2	19	20	29	34	38	41	50
59	60	73	76	78	102	109	121
123	125	128	133	135	137	141	144
149	150	159	166	168	173	176	184
192	194	197	198	221	242	243	249
250	253	254	255	264	275	279	289
298	307	312	313	317	318	319	325
327	329	341	349	377	379	382	393
397	403	410	412	415	417	432	444
450	455	462	466	491	617	627	628
629	634	653	657	667	683	685	688
690	N2	N19	N29	N38	N41	N73	N76
N109	N133	N137	N253	N279	T31	W3	W14
W15	W16						

The Operators

Abellio

Abellio's routes run mostly in south London, but there are exceptions. Route 100 through the City of London is normally an Enviro200 but the odd Dart can appear. 8310 passes the interminable building work in Bevis Marks, between Aldgate and Bishopsgate.

Garages

QB	Battersea
BC	Beddington
BF	Byfleet
TF	Fulwell
WS	Hayes
WL	Walworth

Fleet Total

619

Double Deckers - 303
Single Deckers - 316

PVR = 452

Head Office:
301 Camberwell New Road,
London, SE5 0TF

ROUTES OPERATED

3	35	40	100	112	117	152	156
157	172	188	211	235	322	343	344
350	381	407	414	434	452	481	484
490	931	941	969	C3	C10	H20	H25
H26	H28	N3	N35	N343	N381	P13	R68
R70	U7						

Single Deckers Operated

Dart - ALX200 (ADL)
Dart - Pointer (PDL)
Dart - Pointer 2 (PDL)
E200Dart - Enviro200 (EN/ENL/ENS)
SB120 - Cadet (DWL/DWS)
Citaro G Artic (MA)

Three-quarters of Arriva's London fleet is double-deck, with the Wrightbus integral model much in favour. DW416 is from the 2011 intake, built to the latest ECWVTA specification (see page 46).

Double Deckers Operated

B5LH - Eclipse Gemini 2 (HV)
B7TL - ALX400 (VLA)
B7TL - Eclipse Gemini (VLW)
DB250 - ALX400 (DLA)
DB250 - President (DLP)
DB250 - Pulsar Gemini (DW)
Enviro400 (T)
Gemini 2 DL (DW)
Gemini 2 HEV (HW)

Arriva Southern Counties

Arriva Southern Counties comprises Arriva Kent Thameside and Arriva Southend, both of which have some TfL routes. An early Pulsar Gemini based at Dartford in Kent, comes off the Jolly Farmers roundabout at Crayford.

Garages

DT	Dartford
GY	Grays

Fleet Total

133

Double Deckers - 33
Single Deckers - 100

PVR = 107

Head Office:
Invicta House, Armstrong Road,
Maidstone, Kent ME15 6TY

ROUTES OPERATED

66	126	160	233	256	286	346	370
375	428	492	499	B12	B13	B15	

Single Deckers Operated

Dart - Pointer
Dart - Pointer 2
E200 Dart - Enviro200
SB120 - Cadet
SB120 - MCV

Double Deckers Operated

DB250 Pulsar Gemini
Enviro400

North of the river, Arriva Southend buses based at Grays are entirely single-deckers. An Enviro200 waits at the Gallows Corner Tesco stand.

Arriva The Shires

Garages

WB	High Wycombe
GR	Watford

Fleet Total

92

Double Deckers - 46
Single Deckers - 46

PVR = 73

Head Office:
487 Dunstable Road, Luton,
Bedfordshire LU4 8DS.

Arriva The Shires runs both TfL and non-TfL routes. Red paint differentiates one batch of buses from the other. An SB120 Wrightbus Cadet splashes through Harrow Weald on the circular H19 route.

ROUTES OPERATED

142	258	268	288	303	305	340	640
642	H1	H2	H3	H18	H19	U9	

Single Deckers Operated

Dart - Pointer
Dart - Pointer 2
Optare Solo
SB120 - Cadet

Double Deckers Operated

DB250 - ALX400
DB250 Pulsar Gemini
Gemini 2 HEV
Trident - ALX400

The company has five 7.8 metre Optare Solos working circular trips in Golders Green. On the same damp day, 2468 heads away from Golders Green station on the hourly H3.

CT Plus

Garages

HK   **Ash Grove**
The company is planning to move to Walthamstow shortly.

Fleet Total

83

Double Deckers - 27
Single Deckers - 56

PVR = 63

Head Office:
Mare Street, South Hackney,
London E8.

Hackney Community Transport's CT Plus operates an interesting collection of single- and double-deckers. EO1, for example, is a solitary East Lancs Olympus built onto an Enviro400 chassis. The bus negotiates Threadneedle Street on route 388.

ROUTES OPERATED

153	212	385	388	394	675	W5	W12
W13							

Single Deckers Operated

Dart - Compass (HDC)
Dart - Nimbus (DCS/HDC)
Dart - Pointer (DPS)
E200Dart - Enviro200 (DA/DAS)
E200Dart - Esteem (DE)
Optare Alero (LF)
Optare Solo (OS)

Double Deckers Operated

Enviro400 - Olympus (EO)
N230UD - OmniCity (SD)
Trident - Myllenium Lolyne (HTL)
Trident - President (HTP)

CT Plus has nine Darts with Nimbus bodies for route 394. DCS6 is about to join DCS8 on the stand by the Hospital Tavern at Homerton Hospital.

First

Alexander Dennis's latest products meet at Hornchurch. Enviro200 DML44077 overtakes Enviro400 DN33562. Both are based at Dagenham.

Garages

ON	Alperton
DM	Dagenham
G	Greenford
HS	Hayes
LI	Lea Interchange
NP	Northumberland Park
UX	Uxbridge
X	Westbourne Park
WJ	Willesden Junction

Fleet Total

1147

Double Deckers - 422
Single Deckers - 725

PVR = 929

Head Office:
3rd Floor, Block B, MacMillan House, Paddington, London W2 1TY

ROUTES OPERATED

9	18	23 ●24 hour	25 ●24 hour	26	28	30	31
58	67	79	83 ●24 hour	92	95	165	179
187	191	193	195	207	223	224	226
228	231	236 ●24 hour	245	252	259	282	295 ●24 hour
299	308	309	328	331	339	357	365 ●24 hour
368	389	399	427	476	487	498	607
608	616	646	648	652	656	679	686
692	699	953	A10	E1	E3	E5	E7
E9	E10	N18	N26	N28	N31	N207	PR2
RV1	U1	U2	U3	U4	U5	U10	W4
W10	W11						

Single Deckers Operated

B12T - Excalibur (VCT)
Citaro (ES)
Citaro G Artic (EA)
Dart - Capital (DM/DML/DMS)
Dart - Nimbus (DMC)
E200Dart - Enviro200 (DM/DML/DMS)
SB200 - Pulsar 2 Hydrogen (WSH)

Double Deckers Operated

B7TL - Eclipse Gemini (VNW/VNZ)
B7TL - President (VNL)
B9TL - Eclipse Gemini 2 (VN)
Enviro400 (DN)
Gemini 2 HEV (WNH)
Gemini 2 DL (WN)
Olympian - Palatine (VDN)
Routemaster (RM)
Trident - ALX400 (TNA)
Trident - President (TN/TNL)

President VNL32326 waits time at Aldgate bus station. This is one of a small batch of 17 with the Volvo B7 chassis. The rest of First London's Presidents, roughly 160, have the Trident chassis.

Go-Ahead

The distinctive paint scheme of Go-Ahead London on Silvertown's SE42. Route 300 is operated by the Docklands Buses subsidiary.

Garages

BV	Belvedere
BX	Bexleyheath
Q	Camberwell
MW	Mandela Way
AL	Merton
NX	New Cross
PM	Peckham
PL	Plough Lane
AF	Putney
BE	Rainham
SI	Silvertown
SW	Stockwell
A	Sutton
RA	Waterloo

Fleet Total

1526

Double Deckers - 1039
Single Deckers - 487

PVR = 1306

Head Office:
18 Merton High Strett, London
SW19 1DN

ROUTES OPERATED

1	11	12	14	21	22	24	36
37	39	42	44	45	63	68	74
77	80	85	87	88	89	93	108
118	129	132	151	154	155	163	164
167	170	171	180	185	196	200	201
213	219	225	229	244	270	276	280
300	315	321	333	337	345	347	355
360	362	363	364	376	401	413	422
424	425	430	436	453	468	474	485
486	507	521	549	621	639	649	650
651	655	661	669	670	673	B11	B16
D6	D7	D8	EL1	EL2	G1	N1	N11
N21	N22	N44	N63	N68	N74	N87	N89
N155	N171	N551	P5	P12	W19	X68	

Single Deckers Operated

Citaro (MEC)
Citaro G Artic (MAL)
Dart - Evolution (ED)
Dart - Pointer (DP/LDP)
Dart - Pointer 2 (LDP)
E200Dart - Enviro200 (SE)
E200Dart - Esteem (SOE)
E200Dart - Evolution (ED)
Electrocity (WHY)
N94UB - East Lancs (ELS)
Optare Solo (OS)
SB120 - Cadet (DW)/DWL)

Double Deckers Operated

B7TL - Eclipse Gemini (VWL/WVL)
B7TL - President (PVL/VP)
B7TL - Vyking (EVL)
B9TL - Enviro400 (VE)
B9TL - Eclipse Gemini 2 (WVL)
Enviro400 (E)
Enviro400H (EH)
Enviro400 - Olympus (DOE)
Gemini 2 DL (WDL)
Gemini HEV (WHD)
N94UD OmniDekka (SO)
N230UD OmniCity (SOC)

Go-Ahead had more than 400 Presidents on its books until a clear-out began in 2011. PVL197, for example, here passing Three Kings Pond at Mitcham while working Route 118, was withdrawn only a month after this shot was taken and sent to Ensign Bus for disposal.

London Sovereign

DPS639's driver prepares the bus at Harrow garage. Harrow is a good place to see London Sovereign's Darts as they bustle around the town, many still carrying the older 'grey sandwich' livery.

Garages

BT	Edgware
SO	Harrow

Fleet Total

163

Double Deckers - 65
Single Deckers - 98

PVR = 124

Head Office:
Busways House, Wellington
Road, Fulwell TW2 5NX

ROUTES OPERATED

13	114	183	251	292	324	398	H9
H10	H11	H13	H14	H17	N13		

London Sovereign's other garage at Edgware has twenty Scania OmniCitys, integral buses built in Poland. SP83 heads down Harrow High Street on route 183.

London United

London United's 11.0 metre Vykings can usually be found on the busy route 9. VLE21 negotiates Hyde Park Corner.

Garages

FW	Fulwell
AV	Hounslow
HH	Hounslow Heath
PK	Park Royal
S	Shepherd's Bush
V	Stamford Brook
TV	Tolworth
NC	Twickenham

Fleet Total

886

Double Deckers - 471
Single Deckers - 415

PVR = 701

Head Office:
Busways House, Wellington
Road, Fulwell TW2 5NX

ROUTES OPERATED

9	24 hour 10	24 hour 27	24 hour 33	49	24 hour 57	24 hour 65	71
24 hour 72	81	24 hour 94	110	24 hour 111	116	120	131
24 hour 148	203	216	24 hour 220	222	265	267	272
24 hour 281	283	24 hour 285	290	371	391	419	423
440	482	493	613	665	671	681	691
696	697	698	965	C1	E11	H22	H32
H37	H91	H98	K1	K2	K3	K4	N9
N97							

Single Deckers Operated

Dart - Pointer (DPK)
Dart - Pointer 2 (DP/DPS)
E200Dart - Enviro200 (DE/DLE/SDE)
E200Dart - Enviro200H (HDE)
Optare Tempo (OT)
Optare Versa (OV)

Double Deckers Operated

B7TL - ALX400 (VA)
B7TL - Eclipse Gemini (VR)
B7TL - President (VP)
B7TL - Vyking (VE/VLE)
Enviro400H (ADH)
N94UD OmniCity (SP)
N94UD OmniDekka (SLE)
Trident - ALX400 (TA/TLA)

Park Royal garage has seven of the short (8.9m) Enviro200s for route E11. The other ten of this type operate from Tolworth. SDE17, the last numerically, had just set off on its journey from Greenford.

Metrobus

Metrobus is another part of the Go-Ahead Group, but it's managed from a separate office. Capital-bodied Dart 134 heads along Orpington High Street.

Garages

CY	Crawley
C	Croydon
MB	Orpington

Fleet Total

443

Double Deckers - 152
Single Deckers - 291

PVR = 291

Head Office:
Wheatstone Close, Manor
Royal, Crawley RH10 9UA

ROUTES OPERATED

54	64	75	119	127	130	138	146
161	162	181	202	261	284	293	320
336	352	353	358	359	367	405	464
465	612	654	B14	N64	R1	R2	R3
R4	R5	R6	R7	R8	R9	R10	R11
T32	T33	X26					

Single Deckers Operated

Dart - ALX200
Dart - Capital
Dart - Esteem
Dart - Nimbus
Dart - Pointer
Dart Pointer 2
E200 - Enviro200
MAN 12.240NL - East Lancs
MAN 14.240NL - Enviro200
MAN 14.240NL - Evolution
N94UB OmniCity
N94UB OmniTown
N230UB OmniCity

Double Deckers Operated

N94UD OmniDekka
N230UD - Olympus
N230UD OmniCity
N230UD OmniDekka

Metrobus operates a fascinating variety of single-deckers. A Scania OmniCity single-decker, 523, waits for a driver change opposite the Green Street Green garage (MB). Sixteen of this type are needed to work the 358 service between Orpington and Crystal Palace.

Metroline

More than 70% of Metroline's fleet is double-deck. At Crouch End, the northern terminating point of route 91, TE671 pulls away from the stand and begins another journey into central London. Both this bus, and TE692 parked behind, are from the very first batch of twenty-eight Enviro400s delivered to London at the start of 2006.

Garages

AH	Brentford
W	Cricklewood
EW	Edgware
HD	Harrow Weald
HT	Holloway
KC	Kings Cross
NW	North Wembley
PV	Perivale
PB	Potters Bar
PA	West Perivale
AC	Willesden

Fleet Total

1213

Double Deckers - 873
Single Deckers - 340

PVR = 945

Head Office:
Hygeia House, 66 College Road,
Harrow, Middlesex, HA1 1BE

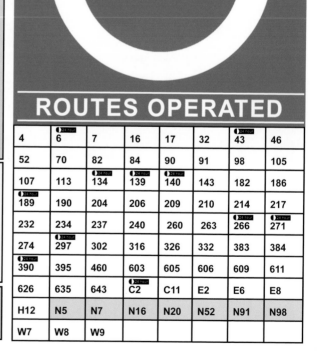

ROUTES OPERATED

4	6 24 hour	7	16	17	32	43 24 hour	46
52	70	82	84	90	91	98	105
107	113	134 24 hour	139 24 hour	140 24 hour	143	182	186
189 24 hour	190	204	206	209	210	214	217
232	234	237	240	260	263	266 24 hour	271 24 hour
274	297 24 hour	302	316	326	332	383	384
390 24 hour	395	460	603	605	606	609	611
626	635	643	C2 24 hour	C11	E2	E6	E8
H12	N5	N7	N16	N20	N52	N91	N98
W7	W8	W9					

Single Deckers Operated

Dart - Pointer (DLD/DLM/DP/DSD)
Dart - Pointer 2 (DLD/DP/DSD)
E200Dart - Enviro200 (DE/DEL/DES)
E200Dart - Evolution (DM)
MAN 12.240 - Evolution (MM)
Optare Tempo Hybrid (OTH)

Double Deckers Operated

B7TL - President (VP/VPL)
B9TL - Eclipse Gemini 2 (VW)
Enviro400 (TE)
Enviro400H (TEH)
N230UD - Olympus (SEL)
Trident - ALX400 (TA/TAL)
Trident - President (TP/TPL)
Volvo Olympian (AV)

Enviro 200 DE994 heads away from Ealing on the E8, a route the type shares with Evolution-bodied E200s and Tempo hybrids. All operate from Brentford garage.

Quality Line

Garages

EB   Epsom

Quality Line now has twelve double-deckers, all of them Enviro400s. They're used on three routes originating from the company's home town of Epsom. DD03 takes a break at Cromwell Road bus station in Kingston.

Fleet Total

75

Double Deckers - 12
Single Deckers - 63

PVR = 57

Head Office:
Blenheim Road, Longmead Est,
Epsom, Surrey KT19 9AF

ROUTES OPERATED

404	406	411	418	463	467	470	641
K5	S1	S3	S4				

Single Deckers Operated

Dart - Nimbus (ET)
Citaro (MCL)
Optare Solo (OP)
Optare Versa (OV)
Dart - ALX200 (SD)
Dart - Esteem (SD)
Dart - East Lancs (SD)
E200Dart - East Lancs (SD)
E200Dart - Enviro 200 (SD)

Double Deckers Operated

Enviro400 (DD)

A selection of Quality Line's single-deckers - an ALX200, SD28, Esteem-bodied Dart SD53 and Enviro200 SD54. All three are taking Sunday off at the Epsom garage.

Stagecoach

One of Stagecoach's innumerable ALX400s departs from Stratford bus station. This is the former site; a new one has recently opened beneath the equally new Westfield shopping centre.

Garages

BK	Barking
TB	Bromley
BW	Bow
TL	Catford
T	Leyton
PD	Plumstead
RM	Rainham
NS	Romford
WH	West Ham

Fleet Total

1320

Double Deckers - 1048
Single Deckers - 272

PVR = 1005

Head Office:
Stephenson Street, Canning Town E16 4SA.

ROUTES OPERATED

5	8	15	47	48	51	53 (24 hour)	55
56	61	62	69 (24 hour)	86	96	97	99
101	103	104	106	115	122	124	136
145	147	158	169	174	175	177	178
199	205 (24 hour)	208	215	227	230	238	241
246	247	248	257	262	269	273	277 (24 hour)
287	291	294	296	314	323	330	354
356	366	372	380	386	387	396	469
472 (24 hour)	473	488	496	541	601	602	624
625	636	637	638	647	658	660	664
672	678	687	D3	N8	N15	N47	N55
N86	N136	N550	P4				

Single Deckers Operated

Dart - ALX200
Dart - Pointer
Dart - Pointer 2
E200 Dart - Enviro200Optare Tempo
Hybrid
Optare Versa

Double Deckers Operated

Enviro400
N230UD OmniCity
Routemaster
Trident - ALX400

The Stagecoach Routemasters operating heritage route 15 are now based at Bow. A solitary passenger enjoys RM2060 at Aldwych.

The Buses

This section looks at the different types of buses you will find on TfL routes - single-deckers first, then double-deckers. For each type we include details of builder, build dates, operators and the routes on which they can be found. However, this is not an exact science. Some garages vary the types they put out on some routes (or do it on all routes!), while others stick religiously to the type nominated in the contract. It goes without saying that failures and non-availability often conspire to produce other interesting workings.

New buses arrive in London every year - 550 double-deckers and more than 240 single-deckers in 2010 alone. When an operator orders a new bus, there are numerous choices to make - what type of chassis, with which engine, what type of axles, which body, seat configuration, style of décor, to name but a few. Some manufacturers offer ready-made packages, but it is perfectly possible to create a fully custom bus. If you've ever ordered a new car from scratch, rather than buying a vehicle already in the dealer's stock, you'll understand how this process works.

Some manufacturers, such as Alexander Dennis Ltd, produce chassis and body. They can either be supplied together (often referred to as an 'integral bus') or the body can be fitted to a chassis built by another maker (and, in ADL's case, *vice versa*). Others concentrate on one or the other. Volvo and VDL (which includes the bus division of the former DAF) produce only chassis. Wrightbus concentrates on bodywork, but now offers what it calls an integral bus even though the chassis components are supplied by VDL.

Optare has been able to supply both chassis and body for single-deckers for the past two years, following the acquisition of East Lancs Coachbuilders but, until now, has relied on other manufacturers' chassis to power its double-deck bodies. At present, the company will only take double-deck orders for niche markets, like open-top sight-seeing buses, but plans to launch its own complete double-deck product (with a Mercedes-Benz engine) within the next 12 months. Scania's latest double-deck offering is an integral bus built in Poland – the OmniCity.

In broad terms, there are only three, or possibly four, double-deck models currently available new to TfL operatiors:

Alexander Dennis Enviro400 (straight diesel or diesel-electric hybrid)
Volvo B9TL/Wrightbus Eclipse Gemini 2 (straight diesel) or Volvo B5LH/Wrightbus Gemini 2 (diesel-electric)
Scania OmniCity CN230UD integral (straight diesel only)
Wrightbus Gemini 2 DL integral (only taken up by Arriva in quantity)

Of all these suppliers, Alexander Dennis has the greatest presence, thanks to the ubiquitous Enviro200 single-decker and the highly-successful

One of two Dart Pointer 2s on loan to Metrobus stops in Green Street Green while providing cover on route 358.

Enviro400. However, competition is fierce: The combination of Volvo B9TL chassis and Wrightbus Gemini 2 body has generated significant orders from TfL operators since 2009, and Volvo has ambitious plans to insert its B9 chassis under a new MCV double-deck body to be built in Egypt (see below). In the single-deck market, only Optare currently offers a challenge to ADL's dominance, although Wrightbus has plans to create a single-decker for London.

On the horizon, the New Bus for London (NBfL), or 'Borismaster' as it's been nicknamed, is currently in development by Wrightbus. The first evaluation vehicle is at the Millbrook test centre in Bedfordshire and six prototypes will go into service in London with Arriva in early 2012. Whether any more of this 'hybrid' three-door, twin staircase bus are built is anyone's guess. The future of the BM will most likely be dictated by politics rather than commercial viability or whether the bus is any good. Mayor Johnson has to face re-election in May 2012 against former Mayor Ken Livingstone (we've discounted the LibDem candidate) and the original scenario envisaged Livingstone regaining office only weeks after his bendybuses were unceremoniously swept away . . . which may be why attempts are being made to bring forward the 'bendy-endy' to December 2011 so it won't look like too much of a coincidence. But, human nature being what it is, and politicians being what they are, what chance would you give the Borismaster if Livingstone is back in post next May? Whatever the outcome in the capital, Wrightbus is gaining huge experience of diesel-electric hybrid technology from the development process and will obviously be keen to promote its new model in modified form for other fleets in the UK and Europe.

The Volvo/MCV double-deck project is equally interesting, but for different reasons. A prototype, VM1, is currently being evaluated by Go-Ahead in east London, mostly on Route 474. Like the first attempt to introduce a similar model, weight continues to be an issue. London Buses' specification calls for a double-decker to carry 87 passengers, either seated or standing. To calculate an accurate laden weight for each bus type, a nominal figure is assigned to each passenger. This has recently been increased from 63.5kg (10 stone) to 68kg (10 stone 10 lbs) per person, which is bad timing for Volvo/MCV. The latest prototype was already overweight, so the bus had to be given special dispensation to operate in London, with its maximum permitted load reduced to 82 passengers. How effectively this problem is addressed will decide whether the type enters service in London in any numbers.

While we're on physical requirements, London Buses also insists that double-deckers have two sets of doors (and most single-deckers), top deck climate control, fire suppression systems and environmentally-friendly exhaust traps. The constant requirement to reduce emissions has enforced tougher and tougher restrictions on builders and operators, and yet another new European standard – known as Euro 6 – will be applied to new orders from the start of 2012.

A Metroline Enviro400 shows off the latest 'colour scheme' for hybrid buses – a white roundel and the 'h'-word displayed discreetly on the flanks.

Obviously, not everything running in the capital is brand-new. Numerous older types can be found, particularly Dennis chassis single-deckers with a host of different bodies. Double-deckers with Dennis, Volvo and DAF chassis remain in abundance, especially with ALX400 and President bodies, and many enthusiasts find these by far the most interesting members of the London fleet. You can even find a trio of East Lancs-bodied Volvo B7s (the remains of London General's EVL class) running alongside a rapidly dwindling number of Plaxton Presidents with centre staircases! And for connoisseurs of the exotic, another unique trio can be found most days on route 85 – the VE class with Enviro400 bodies on Volvo B9TL chassis. These are unique in London and possibly everywhere else.

As we mentioned in the overview, government grants have promoted the introduction of so-called hybrid buses to London's streets – a project that's been taken so seriously that a massive 106 were introduced in the five years to June 2011. That figure is likely to double by the start of 2012, but progress is best described as pitiful when there are more than 8,000 buses working TfL contracts. The chart below shows introduction dates for the current fleet of hybrids and lists the models on order. We have also included the hydrogen fuel cell buses, even though the technology has so far proved a little tetchy.

Government grants – the so-called Green Fund – have now been used up, which means the extra cost of hybrid models will have to be fully borne by TfL operators in future. So far, only Go-Ahead has committed itself to this course with 15 hybrids included in the route 19 conversion, and Abellio for its renewed contract on route 3 – both scheduled for March 2012. Whether this is genuinely the start of a new trend, only time will tell.

Date Introduced	Type	No.	Operator	Route Worked	Running Numbers	Notes
Feb '06	Electrocity	6	Go-Ahead	360	WHY1-6	
Nov '07	Electrocity	5	Travel London	129	8801-5	now Abellio, but not route 129
Mar '08	Electrocity	1	Go-Ahead	360	WHY7	
Dec '08	Enviro400	5	Metroline	16	TEH915-919	
Dec '08	Gemini 2	1	Go-Ahead	24	WHD1	
Dec '08	Tempo	5	Stagecoach	276	29001-5	re-numbered to 25111-5
Dec '08	Dec '08	1	Go-Ahead	24	EH1	
Jan '09	Enviro400	4	Go-Ahead	24	EH2-5	
Jan '09	Gemini 2	5	First	328	WNH39001-5	
Jan '09	Gemini 2	5	Arriva	141	HW1-5	delivered Jan - Apr '09
Jan '09	Enviro400	2	London United	482	ADH1-2	
Apr '09	Enviro200	5	London United	371	HDE1-5	
Jun '09	Gemini 2	6	Arriva	141	HV1-6	now working route 76
Jul '09	Tempo	5	Metroline	E8	OTH971-5	
Nov '10	Enviro400	20	London United	94	ADH3-22	
Nov '10	Gemini 2	20	Arriva	76	HV7-26	delivered Nov '10 - Feb '11
Feb '11	Hydrogen bus	5	First	RV1	WSH62991-5	
Jul '11	Gemini 2	20	Arriva	73	HV27-46	
On Order	Hydrogen bus	3	First	RV1	WSH62996-8	
On Order	Enviro400	13	Abellio	188	2001-13	
On Order	Enviro400	26	Metroline	16/139	TEH1217-42	
On Order	Gemini 2	16	Go-Ahead	453	WHV1-16	
On Order	Enviro400	15	Go-Ahead	436	EH6-20	
On Order	Electrocity	6	Go-Ahead	360	WHY8-13	
On Order	Enviro400	26	Stagecoach	15	12128-12153	
On Order	Enviro400	22	Abellio	3	2014-2035	

Wrightbus Integrals / ECWVTA

Confusion often arises over the so-called integral vehicles supplied by Wrightbus to Arriva London, and elsewhere. Wright's original double-decker was known as a DAF DB250LF/Wrightbus Pulsar Gemini – the Arriva batch numbered from DW1-DW50.

DAF was then acquired by VDL Groep in Holland and the chassis became known as the VDL DB250LF (Arriva batch DW51-DW133). Concurrently a version of the same double-deck body was available with the Volvo B7TL chassis, and known as a Wrightbus Eclipse Gemini – probably the start of the confusion. This combination was supplied in large quantities to London operators other than Arriva.

In 2009, Wright began supplying an updated double-decker, described as the Gemini 2 DL Integral. The DL is short for diesel. Although this version used the updated VDL DB300LF chassis, it was described as an integral bus "built with VDL components", whereas the later Volvo-powered version of the revamped Gemini body has always been described as a Volvo B9TL/Eclipse Gemini 2 – no use of the word integral, no 'DL', no wonder there's confusion.

A solitary Gemini 2 DL (WDL1) was supplied to Go-Ahead for evaluation alongside a Wrightbus hybrid (WHD1), four more went to First London (WN35001-4), but the bulk orders came from Arriva again. DW201-onwards appeared throughout 2009/10 and were initially used for the conversion of route 38 to double-deck operation. Deliveries of these integrals continued up to DW336, whereupon something different happened.

DW337 was built to a new European design directive known as ECWVTA – European Community Whole Vehicle Type Approval. The updated bus was exhibited at the NEC bus & coach show in November 2010, but it then scurried back to the Ballymena factory for "more work". It was finally delivered to Arriva London at the start of May 2011, numbered DW401, and put to work on either route 38 or route 242.

Many of the ECWVTA alterations are mechanical items out-of-sight beneath the bus body, but the visible alterations are sets of amber marker lights along the lower bodysides and additional amber lights by the centre doors on the nearside, which provide a flashing warning when the wheelchair ramp is in use. The emergency door in the rear off-side of the lower deck has also been dispensed with, in favour of break glass and hammers (!) Externally these alterations are the only way to distinguish the latest intake from the DW201 batch, apart from the running numbers. Deliveries from DW402-onwards (still in progress) have also been built to the ECWVTA spec, as has the Volvo/MCV trials bus VM1.

The new regulations will now apply to everything, as the long-standing type approval system for passenger-carrying vehicles, known as a UK Certificate of Initial Fitness, ceases to have any effect from October 24th 2011.

Before another myth arises, there is no direct connection, as such, between integrals and ECWVTA. It is simply a matter of timing that Arriva's latest buses are the first to be built to this spec.

Before another myth . . . 2: The deep padded seats fitted to DW401 onwards are nothing to do with ECWVTA, merely a comfort bonus for Arriva's passengers.

Single-Deckers

Citaro 12.0m

MEC2 heads along Angel Street at the back of St. Paul's. Go-Ahead has fifty of these based at Waterloo garage (code RA, dating back to the original Red Arrow services). The modern-day 'red arrows' work routes 507 & 521, both formerly operated with Mercedes artics.

Built: **Mercedes-Benz**   Introduced: **2009**   Number: **56**
Operators (routes): **Go-Ahead (507, 521), London United (203)**

Citaro G (Artic) 18.0m

The aforementioned artics are due to disappear from London streets by the end of 2011 (if the route 207 replacement is brought forward). Arriva's MA11 makes the last stop along route 29 in Trafalgar Square before going to the Northumberland Avenue stand.

Built: **Mercedes-Benz**   Introduced: **2002-2005 & 2008**   Number: **159**
Operators (routes): **Arriva (29), First (207), Go-Ahead (12, 436, 453)**

Dart - ALX200 8.9m

A pair of Quality Line ALX200s, SD27 & SD28, at their Epsom depot. These buses are nominally allocated to route S3, but there is an element of 'mix & match' with other types day-to-day.

Built by: **Dennis/Alexander**   Introduced: **2000 & 2001**   Number: **18**
Operators (routes): **Quality Line (S3), Stagecoach (124, 273, 380)**

Dart - ALX200 9.4m

A battered-looking ADL66 heads away from Walthamstow. Nineteen of these remain, all based at Edmonton garage.

Built by: **Dennis/Alexander**   Introduced: **2000**   Number: **19**
Operators (routes): **Arriva (397, 410, 444, W14, W15)**

Dart - ALX200 10.2m

ADL981 sets off from Homerton Hospital. This is one of three of this combination based at Ash Grove, out of Arriva's total stock of fifteen.

Built by: **Dennis/Alexander**   Introduced: **1998 & 2001**   Number: **51**
Operators (routes): **Arriva (78, W15), Stagecoach (366)**

Dart - ALX200 10.8m

Only Stagecoach still operates the longer ALX200. 34340 appears at Homerton only weeks before Stagecoach lost route 276 to Go-Ahead.

Built by: **Dennis/Alexander**   Introduced: **2001**   Number: **18**
Operators (routes): **Stagecoach (323)**

Dart - Capital 8.9m

Metrobus's 133 waits at the stand in Green Street Green. The company operates fifteen of these in the Orpington area.

Built by: **Dennis/Marshall, TransBus/Marshall**   Introduced: **1999-2002**   Number: **30**
Operators (routes): **First (193), Metrobus (R1, R3, R4, R6)**

Dart - Capital 9.3m

DM41434 approaches Walthamstow greyhound stadium. This variant of the Dart can be found in east and west London.

Built by: **Dennis/Marshall**   Introduced: **1999-2002**   Number: **48**
Operators (routes): **First (223, 299, 309, 357, 389, 399, PR2 W10, W11)**

Dart - Capital 10.2m

The longest version is 10.2 metres. DML41772 waits at Scrattons Farm Estate alongside the A13 in Dagenham, before working the Wednesday only 953 back to Romford.

Built by: **Dennis/Marshall**   Introduced: **1998-2001**   Number: **51**
Operators (routes): **First (224, 236, 308, 646, 953), Metrobus (R1, R9)**

Dart - Compass 10.7m

The only Dennis Dart/Caetano Compass running in the capital is this one. HDC12, operated by CT Plus, can usually be found on route 153.

Built by: **Dennis/Caetano**   Introduced: **1999**   Number: **1**
Operators (routes): **CT Plus (153)**

Dart - Esteem 9.0m

Metrobus 230 amid the leafy splendour of Oakwood Avenue in Beckenham. Very few single door buses remain in the TfL area.

Built by: **Alexander Dennis/East Lancs**   Introduced: **2006**   Number: **21**
Operators (routes): **Metrobus (138, 146, 336, 367)**

Dart - Evolution 9.2m

Go-Ahead has a fleet of nine of these working between Walthamstow and Ilford. ED13 heads along Essex Road South in Waltham Forest.

Built by: **Alexander Dennis/MCV**   Introduced: **2006**   Number: **9**
Operators (routes): **Go-Ahead (W19)**

Dart - Evolution 10.4m

From the following batch, Go-Ahead's ED19 runs past the roadworks in Barking Road, Newham.

Built by: **Alexander Dennis/MCV**   Introduced: **2007**   Number: **11**
Operators (routes): **Go-Ahead (300)**

Dart - Evolution 10.8m

The longest version of the Evolution is 10.8 metres. Go-Ahead currently has eight - two at New Cross, two at Silvertown, and four out of service. Photo: Jack Marian

Built by: **Alexander Dennis/MCV**   Introduced: **2006**   Number: **8**
Operators (routes): **Go-Ahead (108, 129)**

Dart - Myllennium 9m

Although officially allocated to work the S3, Quality Line's five Myllenniums regularly turn out on other routes. SD39 is about to depart from Asda at Beddington on route 463. Photo: Brian Kemp

Built by: **Alexander Dennis/East Lancs**   Introduced: **2005**   Number: **5**
Operators (routes): **Quality Line (S3)**

Dart - Nimbus 8.9m

CT Plus's nine buses of this type work route 394 alongside Enviro200s. DCS8 begins its journey to Islington. In the background DCS5 stands outside Homerton Hospital.

Built by: **TransBus/Caetano** Introduced: **2002 & 2003** Number: **9**
Operators (routes): **CT Plus (394)**

Dart - Nimbus 10.5m

The longer two-door Nimbus is more common - Abellio's 8468 rests in an arboreal setting at Haven Green, Ealing.

Built by: **Dennis/Caetano, TransBus/Caetano, Alexander Dennis/Caetano**
Introduced: **2001-04** Number: **84**
Operators (routes): **Abelio (112, 490, 941, 969, H25, U1, U2, U3, U5, U10), CT Plus (153), First (236, 308, D8)**

Dart - Nimbus 11.0m

Only Abellio operates the 11 metre Nimbus and all are based at Twickenham. 8737 is about to depart from the County Court terminus in Brentford. The work of route 235 is shared by 10.2m Pointers.

Built by: **TransBus/Caetano**   Introduced: **2003**   Number: **12**
Operators (routes): **Abellio (235)**

Dart - Pointer 8.8m

The 8.8m Pointer is known as a Mini Pointer. Metrobus's 273 takes a break at Sainsbury's in Lower Sydenham.

Built by: **Dennis/Plaxton, Dennis/Alexander, TransBus, Alexander Dennis**
Introduced: **2000/2002 - 2006**   Number: **142**
Operators (routes): **Abellio (322, 481, H20, H28, P13), Arriva (318, 327, 377, 379, 382, W16), Arriva the Shires (U9), CT Plus (385), Go-Ahead (315, 424, G1), Metrobus (352, 464, R1, R5, R7, R10, R11), Stagecoach (124, 380)**

Dart - Pointer 9.2m

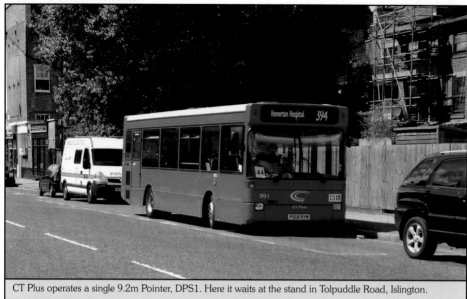

CT Plus operates a single 9.2m Pointer, DPS1. Here it waits at the stand in Tolpuddle Road, Islington.

Built by: **Dennis/Plaxton**   Introduced: **1996**   Number: **3**
Operators (routes): **Go-Ahead (360), CT Plus (394)**

Dart - Pointer 9.3m

Arriva has the largest number of this variant - thirty-five. PDL124 is between trips at Lower Sydenham.

Built by: **TransBus, Alexander Dennis**   Introduced: **2002/03/06**   Number: **53**
Operators (routes): **Arriva (397, 444, 450, W14, W15), Metroline (W9), Stagecoach (291, 386)**

Dart - Pointer 10.1m

The most numerous of the Pointers are the 10.1 metre variety. 34364 sits in the yard opposite Bromley garage.

Built by: **Dennis/Plaxton, TransBus, Alexander Dennis**   Introduced: **2000/2002 & 2003**   Number: **139**
Operators (routes): **Abelio (152, 235, 490, 917, 931 U7), Arriva (166, 312) Go-Ahead (39, 80, 108, 132, 164, 201, 219, 225, 413, 485), London United (110), Metroline (209, 232), Stagecoach (314, 366, P4)**

Dart - Pointer 10.7m

A London General-branded 10.7m Pointer, DP204, has just passed Sutton garage while working the 413. The bus is based at Stockwell.

Built by: **TransBus**   Introduced: **2003 & 2004**   Number: **32**
Operators (routes): **Go-Ahead (170, 347, 413), Metrobus (130, 359)**

Dart - Pointer 2 8.8m

PDL59 crosses the busy junction of Cranbrook Road and High Road in Ilford.

Built by: **Dennis/Plaxton**   Introduced: **2000 & 2001**   Number: **56**
Operators (routes): **Abelio (H28), Arriva (462), Go-Ahead (424), London United (K4)**

Dart - Pointer 2 9.3m

A London Central-branded Pointer 2, LDP188, passes Pimilco station while standing in for an unavailable Electrocity on route 360.

Built by: **Dennis/Plaxton, Alexander Dennis**   Introduced: **1999/01/04/05**   Number: **25**
Operators (routes): **Go-Ahead (P12), Stagecoach (291)**

Dart - Pointer 2 10.1m

One of twenty-seven Pointer 2s operated by London Sovereign (Transdev), DPS511 takes Sunday off in the yard at Harrow garage.

Built by: **Dennis/Plaxton, TransBus, Alexander Dennis**   Introduced: **1997-2004/06**   Number: **297**
Operators (routes): **Abelio (152), Go-Ahead (355, 360), London Sovereign (398, H9, H10, H11, H13, H14, H17), London United (110, 116, 203, 216, 265, 290, 371, 419, 665, H22, H37, K2, K3), Metroline (46, 70, 90, 117, 206, 209, 214, 232, 234, 274, C11), Stagecoach (178)**

Dart - Pointer 2 10.7m

Go-Ahead's Blue Triangle operates out of Rainham in Essex. DP209 stands in front of the fuel tanks in the garage yard.

Built by: **Dennis/Plaxton, Alexander Dennis**   Introduced: **1998-2000/06**   Number: **118**
Operators (routes): **Arriva (78, 255, 289), Arriva Kent Thameside (126), Go-Ahead (347, 367), London United (222), Metrobus (130, T33)**

Dart - Pointer 2 11.3m

The longest Pointer 2s are the 11.3 metre version operated by Stagecoach. All are allocated to route 227 from Bromley to Crystal Palace. 34226 in Bromley Road, Beckenham.

Built by: **Dennis/Plaxton**
Operators (routes): **Stagecoach (227)**

Introduced: **2000**

Number: **13**

Dart - Spryte 10.3m

There are only four of these and you need to travel to west London to see them. They work route U7 between Hayes and Uxbridge. 8419 is about to depart from the former.

Built by: **Dennis/East Lancs**   Introduced: **2000**   Number: **4**
Operators (routes): **Abelio (U7)**

E200Dart - Enviro200 8.9m

The Enviro200 design is now the single-decker of choice for most operators. Abellio's 8107 soaks up the sun at Beddington garage.

Built: **Alexander Dennis**   Introduced: **2006-11**   Number: **159**
Operators (routes): **Abelio (434, 481, H26), Arriva (192), Arriva Kent & Thameside (233), Ct Plus (394), First (E5, E10, W4), London Sovereign, London United (324, 965, E11, K1), Metrobus (162B14), Metroline (383, 384, W9), Quality Ilne (S3), Stagecoach (273, 314, 354, 356)**

E200Dart - Enviro200 9.3m

40 centimetres separate the previous type and this one. Abellio's 8322 passes two famous London landmarks on route 100.

Built: **Alexander Dennis**   Introduced: **2007-2011**   Number: **68**
Operators (routes): **Abelio (100, 484), Arriva (393), First (339), Go-Ahead (P5), Stagecoach (291, 386)**

E200Dart - Enviro200 10.2m

The most common Enviro200 is the 10.2 metre version. 8531 turns into George Street, Richmond.

Built: **Alexander Dennis**   Introduced: **2007-2011**   Number: **704**
Operators (routes): **Abelio (117, 152, 350, 407, 917, 931, C10, R68, R70), Arriva (166, 173, 184, 312, 325, 491, T31), Arriva Kent Thameside (B12), Arriva Southend (370, 375, 499), First (95, 165, 187, 195, 226, 228, 245, 331, 487, 498, 646, A10, D6, E7, E9, RV1, U1, U2, U3, U5, U10), Go-Ahead (167, 200, 244, 300, 549 B11, B16), London Sovereign (251, 398, H9, H10, H11, H13, H14, H17), London United (33, 72, 216, 272, 285, 371, 440, 493, C1), Metrobus (465), Metroline (143, 190, 316, 326, 395, C11, E6, E8), Stagecoach (62, 296, 323, 488, D3)**

E200Dart - Enviro200 10.8m

Another of the long 200s, Blue Triangle's Rainham-based SE29, passes Ilford railway station.

Built: **Alexander Dennis**   Introduced: **2007-2011**   Number: **124**
Operators (routes): **Arriva Kent Thameside (286, 428), Arriva Southend (66), Go-Ahead (170, 276, 347, 362, 364), London United (423, H98), Metroline, Stagecoach (246)**

E200Dart - Enviro200H 10.2m

There are only five diesel-electric hybrid Enviro200s in operation, working route 371 in south-west London. HDE1 pulls away from the stop by Richmond bus stand.

Built: **Alexander Dennis**   Introduced: **2009**   Number: 5
Operators (routes): **London United (371)**

E200Dart - Esteem 9.4m

The Enviro200 chassis has also been used with non-ADL bodies. DE6 is one of six working for CT Plus with an Esteem body.

Built: **Alexander Dennis/East Lancs**   Introduced: **2007**   Number: **6**
Operators (routes): **CT Plus (W13)**

E200Dart - Esteem 9.5m

Quality Line has nine mid-length Esteems. SD46 at the Mitcham stand of route S1.

Built: Alexander **Dennis/East Lancs**   Introduced: **2007**   Number: **9**
Operators (routes): **Quality Line (S1, S4)**

E200Dart - Esteem 10.4m

The newest Esteem-bodied Enviro200s were delivered to Go-Ahead in 2009. A fleet of forty is split between Merton & Sutton. This is Sutton's SOE36 leaving Morden on route 80.

Built: **Alexander Dennis/Optare**   Introduced: **2009**   Number: **40**
Operators (routes): **Go-Ahead (80, 163, 164, 200, 219, 355, 413)**

E200Dart - Evolution 10.4m

MCV Evolution bodies can also be found on the Enviro200 chassis, like Metroline's DM969, here taking a break at Richmond. The clunky white box on the roof is the air-conditioning unit.

Built: **Alexander Dennis/MCV**   Introduced: **2009**   Number: **10**
Operators (routes): **Metroline (E8, 190)**

Electrocity 10.3m

The seventh of Go-Ahead's Electrocitys is the only 10.3m version. WHY7 calls at Vauxhall bus station while on its regular route 360.

Built: **Wrightbus**　　　　　　　Introduced: **2007 & 2008**　　　　　　　Number: **6**
Operators (routes): **Abelio (100), Go-Ahead (360)**

Electrocity 10.4m

The first six, like WHY5 here, are longer by a whole centimetre. They reappeared on route 360 in May 2011 after extensive rebuilding by Wrightbus in Ballymena.

Built: **Wrightbus**　　　　　　　Introduced: **2005 & 2006**　　　　　　　Number: **6**
Operators (routes): **Go-Ahead (360)**

MAN 12.240 - Evolution 10.4m

MAN has also supplied the occasional chassis for Evolution bodies. MM812 heads away from Wood Green on the High Road. All of these work for Metroline.

Built: **MAN/MCV**   Introduced: **2007**   Number: **38**
Operators (routes): **Metroline (90, 206, 232)**

MAN 12.240NL - East Lancs 10.3m

Metrobus operates a fleet of five MANs with East Lancs bodies on route R2. 701 heads away from Biggin Hill.

Built: **MAN/East Lancs**   Introduced: **2007**   Number: **5**
Operators (routes): **Metrobus (R2)**

MAN 14.240NL - Enviro200 10.7m

Metrobus Enviro-bodied MAN, 706, nears its destination on King Henry's Drive, New Addington.

Built: **MAN/Alexander Dennis**   Introduced: **2008**   Number: **3**
Operators (routes): **Metrobus (359, T32)**

MAN 14.240NL - Evolution 10.8m

More Metrobus MAN power: All fifteen of these are based at the Beddington Lane Croydon garage for working route 202. 709 approaches Lee station.

Built: **MAN/MCV**   Introduced: **2009**   Number: **15**
Operators (routes): **Metrobus (202)**

N94UB - East Lancs 10.6m

East Lancs-bodied Scania ELS7 in the Aldgate one-way system while working route 42. Fourteen of these are garaged at Camberwell.

Built: **Scania/East Lancs**   Introduced: **2002**   Number: **14**
Operators (routes): **Go-Ahead (42)**

N94UB - Esteem 10.6m

Metrobus Esteem-bodied Scanias can be found working routes 181 & 284 between Grove Park & Lewisham. All are based at Orpington. 608 approaches Grove Park station.

Built: **Scania/East Lancs**   Introduced: **2006**   Number: **23**
Operators (routes): **Metrobus (181, 284)**

N94UB OmniCity 12m

Metrobus are the only operators of the SN94UD Scania OmniCity single-decker. 528 heads through Bromley.

Built: **Scania**   Introduced: **2002-2005**   Number: **46**
Operators (routes): **Metrobus (46, 358, X26)**

N230UB OmniCity 12m

The N230UB Scania OmniCity is also operated only by Metrobus. 566 pulls into Kingston bus station while working the limited stop X26 service.

Built: **Scania**   Introduced: **2007-09**   Number: **23**
Operators (routes): **Metrobus (293, X26)**

SB120 - Cadet 9.4m

Arriva Southern Counties has twelve of the DAF SB120/Wrightbus Cadet combination based at Dartford. 3945 at New Eltham.

Built: **DAF/Wrightbus**   Introduced: **2003 & 2004**   Number: **42**
Operators (routes): **Arriva (410), Arriva Southern Counties (428, B13, B15), Go-Ahead (132, 201)**

SB120 - Cadet 10.2m

Arriva the Shires has eighteen of the longer version based at Watford. 3727 turns into Harrow High Street.

Built: **DAF/Wrightbus, VDL/Wrightbus**   Introduced: **2001-2003/06**   Number: **84**
Operators (routes): **Arriva (255, 289, 298, 313, 444, 455, W15), Arriva Southend (256, 346, 499), Arriva the Shires (288, 303, 305, H18, H19)**

SB120 - Cadet 10.8m

Two operators have the 10.8m Cadet in their fleet. Arriva's six work on the north London route 313. DWL25 pauses at Ponders End.

Built: **DAF/Wrightbus, VDL/Wrightbus**   Introduced: **2002 & 2004**   Number: **31**
Operators (routes): **Arriva (313), Go-Ahead (108, 132)**

SB200 - Pulsar 2 (Hydrogen Fuel Cell) 11.9m

First London's WSH62992 is one of five hydrogen fuel cell buses undergoing trials on route RV1. There should be eight by now, but the fleet has been a little intermittent because of technical issues.

Built: **VDL/Wrightbus**   Introduced: **2010 & 2011**   Number: **5**
Operators (routes): **First (RV1)**

Solo 7.8m

Arriva The Shires has five short Solos for trips around the Golders Green area. 2472 has just completed a circuit of Hampstead Garden Suburb and is returning in the rain to Golders Green.

Built: **Optare**
Operators (routes): **Arriva the Shires (H1, H2, H3)**

Introduced: **2006 & 2007**

Number: **6**

Solo 8.5m

Quality Line runs a fleet of twenty-one 8.5m Solos. OP19 stands outside the Epsom garage.

Built: **Optare**   Introduced: **2001-2003**   Number: **28**
Operators (routes): **Quality Line (404, 470, S4)**

Solo 8.8m

The shorter Solos are augmented by eight of the 8.8m version. OP28 head for Pollards Hill on Croydon road, Wallington, while working its regular route.

Built: **Optare**   Introduced: **2009 & 2011**   Number: **18**
Operators (routes): **CT Plus (W5), Quality Line (463)**

Solo SE 7.1m

The shortest buses in London are the two 7.1 metre Solos working for Metrobus. They're used on the narrow lanes to and from Biggin Hill. However, on this occasion 101 has escaped onto route R5 at Green Street Green.

Built: **Optare**   Introduced: **2006**   Number: **2**
Operators (routes): **Metrobus (R8)**

Solo SE 7.8m

CT Plus has seven Solos for route W12, running between Walthamstow and Wanstead in east London. OS6 has just arrived at its destination.

Built: **Optare**   Introduced: **2010**   Number: **7**
Operators (routes): **CT Plus (W12)**

Tempo 12.0m

New to London in 2011 were sixteen London United 12m Optare Tempos based at Hounslow Kingsley Road. OT2 crosses Richmond Bridge.

Built: **Optare**   Introduced: **2011**   Number: **16**
Operators (routes): **London United (H37)**

Tempo Hybrid 10.6m

Metroline operates Optare Tempo hybrids on route E8 in west London. OTH974 heads for Ealing Broadway at Northfields.

Built: **Optare**   Introduced: **2008 & 2009**   Number: **5**
Operators (routes): **Metroline (E8)**

Versa 10.4m

Stagecoach's Optare Versa 25310 heads towards Gants Hill along Cranbrook Road while working route 396.

Built: **Optare**   Introduced **2008 & 09**   Number: **50**
Operators (routes): **London United (283, 391), Stagecoach (396, 469)**

Versa 11.1m

Quality Line's eight 11.1m Versas can be found on route 411. OV3 has just made its penultimate stop outside the Kingston branch of John Lewis before heading to Cromwell Road bus station.

Built: **Optare**   Introduced: **2010**   Number: **8**
Operators (routes): **Quality Line (411)**

Double-Deckers

B5LH - Eclipse Gemini 2 10.4m

Arriva is the only London operator with this model of hybrid. HV2 passes a deserted Bank junction while working route 76 early one Saturday.

Built: **Volvo/Wrightbus**   Introduced: **2009-2011**   Number: **46**
Operators (routes): **Arriva (73, 76, 149, 243)**

B7TL - ALX400 10.1m

The B7TL-fitted ALX400s can be quite noisy . . . if you get a good one. VA300 waits time on the Bolinbroke Road stand at Clapham Junction, still showing off the rebellious Transdev livery.

Built: **Volvo/Alexander, Volvo/TransBus**   Introduced: **2000/02/03**   Number: **164**
Operators (routes): **Arriva (123, 128, 159, 249, 415, 432), London United (27, 49, 81, 111, 120, 148, 220, 222, 696, 697, H32)**

B7TL - ALX400 10.6m

One of Arriva's longer Volvo-powered ALX400s, VLA20, heads out of Brixton followed by Abellio's Enviro400 9464.

Built: **Volvo/TransBus, Volvo/Alexander Dennis**   Introduced: **2003-2005**   Number: **73**
Operators (routes): **Arriva (2, 176, 415, 417)**

B7TL - Eclipse Gemini 10.1m

The original Eclipse Gemini is Wrightbus's most numerous design working in London. Arriva's VLW120 is about to move off from Enfield garage to work route 349.

Built: **Volvo/Wrightbus**   Introduced: **2001-2005**   Number: **541**
Operators (routes): **Arriva (141, 144, 168, 221, 242, 253, 254, 275, 279, 349, 468, 667, W3), First (28, 31, 79, 83 328), Go-Ahead (14, 22, 44, 45, 68, 74, 77, 85, 87, 88, 118, 155, 180, 270, 280, 333, 430, 639, 655, 669, 670, X68), London United (11)**

Volvo-powered Gemini 9023 takes a breather at Aldgate bus station before returning south of the river. It's rare these days to see anything but an Enviro400 on route 40.

Built: **Volvo/Wrightbus**   Introduced: **2002-2006**   Number: 164
Operators (routes): **Abelio (40, 157, 188, 343, 350, 381), Arriva (253, 254), First (92), Go-Ahead (1, 185, 669)**

B7TL - Myllennium Vyking 10.4m

One of London United's three 10.4m Vykings, VE3, waits for its next job at Shepherds Bush garage.

Built: **Volvo/East Lancs**   Introduced: **2002 & 2004**   Number: **13**
Operators (routes): **Go-Ahead (87), London United (49)**

B7TL - Myllennium Vyking 11.0m

The 11m Myllennium Vykings were split between London United (RATP) and London Soverign (Transdev) in the March 2011 asset realignment. The buses allocated to Turnham Green, normally found on route 9, are being refurbished, like VLE20 captured here between journeys at Aldwych.

Built: **Volvo/East Lancs**   Introduced: **2004**   Number: **45**
Operators (routes): **London Sovereign (13, 114, 183, 292), London United (9, 27)**

B7TL - President 10.0m

Despite the clear-out in 2011, Go-Ahead retains a large number of B7TL/Presidents. Sutton's PVL297 restarts from the small Wimbledon bus station.

Built: **Volvo/Plaxton, Volvo/TransBus, Volvo/Alexander Dennis**
Introduced: **2000-2005**   Number: **572**
Operators (routes): **Go-Ahead (21, 22, 36, 44, 45, 63, 68, 77, 87, 88, 89, 93, 118, 151, 154, 155, 171, 185, 200, 213, 270, 280, 321, 333, 345, 363, 401, 425, 468, 621, 639, 649, 650, 651, 655, 661, 669, 670, 673, X68), London United (81, 120, 696, 687, H32), Metroline (4, 6, 43, 98, 134, 140, 182, 260, 271, 302, 460, C2, H12, W7)**

B7TL - President 10.6m

Metroline's 10.6 metre President, VP622, turns into Harrow High Street on route 140.

Built: **Volvo/Plaxton, Volvo/TransBus, Volvo/Alexander Dennis**
Introduced: **2000-2005**   Number: **160**
Operators (routes): **First (67, 259, 476), London Sovereign (13, 114, 183, 292), Metroline (4, 6, 17, 43, 52, 107, 113, 134, 140, 182, 186, 240, 390, 605, 606)**

B9TL - Eclipse Gemini 2 10.4m

Go-Ahead operates routes EL1 & EL2 with Eclipse Gemini 2s on the Volvo B9TL chassis. A number are painted in a distinctive colour scheme, like WVL349 at Ilford.

Built: **Volvo/Wrightbus**   Introduced: **2009-2011**   Number: **453**
Operators (routes): **First (18, 25, 58, 79, 83, 259, 427, 476, 486), Go-Ahead (21, 37, 63, 89, 171, 229, 363, 401, 422, 474, EL1, EL2), Metroline (237, E2)**

B9TL - Enviro400 10.4m

The three VolvoB9TL/Enviro400 combinations in London are operated by Go-Ahead from Putney garage on route 85. VE2 waits time at the 'country end' stand in Kingston Hall Road.

Built: **Volvo/Alexander Dennis**   Introduced: **2008**   Number: **3**
Operators (routes): **Go-Ahead (85)**

The newest design to reach London is Volvo/MCV double-decker VM1. Go-Ahead is evaluating this design from its Docklands Buses garage at Silvertown in east London, usually on route 474 but sometimes the 425.

Built: **Volvo/MCV**　　　　　Introduced: **2011**　　　　　Number: **1**
Operators (routes): **Go-Ahead (474)**

CN94UD OmniCity 10.7m

London United is the only operator with this particular combination. Eleven, including SP13, are based at Hounslow, the other four at Hounslow Heath.

Built: **Scania**   Introduced: **2006**   Number: **15**
Operators (routes): **London United (81, 120, 698)**

DB250LF - ALX400 10.2m

Arriva the Shires' DB250LF/ALX400 6003 pulls out of Harrow High Street.

Built: **DAF/Alexander, DAF/TransBus**   Introduced: **1999-2003**   Number: **278**
Operators (routes): **Arriva (20, 34, 41, 50, 59, 60, 76, 109, 123, 141, 176, 194, 197, 198, 243, 249, 250, 253, 254, 279, 289, 317, 319, 412, 415, 432, 466, 657, 685, 690, W3), Arriva the Shires (142, 340, 642)**

DB250LF - ALX400 10.6m

Arriva is the sole operator of this combination in 10.6m length. Numbers are dwindling, but some are likely to continue as training vehicles. DLA20 crosses London Bridge while on route 121.

Built: **DAF/Alexander**   Introduced: **1998 & 1999**   Number: **42**
Operators (routes): **Arriva (121, 144, 198, 221, 250, 279, 349, 617, 628, 653, 667, 688)**

DB250LF - President 10.2m

Yet another combo solely operated by Arriva. DLP85 approaches its home garage at Ponders End, Enfield, on route 307.

Built: **DAF/TransBus**   Introduced: **2002**   Number: **15**
Operators (routes): **Arriva (279, 307, 349)**

DB250LF - President 10.6m

DLP56 heads a line-up of Presidents inside Palmers Green garage. Thirty-five are based here, twenty at Enfield, and a solitary example at Wood Green.

Built: **DAF/Plaxton**   Introduced: **1999 & 2001**   Number: **56**
Operators (routes): **Arriva (125, 144, 221, 279, 329, 629, 634, 683, W3)**

DB250LF - Pulsar Gemini 10.3m

Still sporting its white horns, Arriva's DW121 passes the horse head at Marble Arch. Route 159 is normally operated by ALX400s or Gemini 2 Wrightbuses.

Built: **DAF/Wrightbus, VDL/Wrightbus**   Introduced: **2003-2006**   Number: **161**
Operators (routes): **Arriva (19, 50, 59, 60, 137, 159, 194, 264, 403, 412, 466, 627, 685), Arriva Kent Thameside (492), Arriva the Shires (258)**

Enviro400 10.1m

First London's first London Enviro - DN33501 approaches Ilford station on route 179.

Built: **Alexander Dennis**   Introduced: **2005-2011**   Number: **1029**
Operators (routes): **Abelio (35, 40, 156, 344, 414, 452, N35), Arriva (50, 78, 102, 109, 133, 135, 150, 168, 197, 198, 242, 250, 329, 341, 466, 629, 634), Arriva Southern Counties (160), Arriva the Shires (642) First (23, 26, 30, 105, 179, 191, 213, 231, 252, 282, E1, E3), Go-Ahead (24, 36, 37, 63, 88, 93, 118, 151, 196, 333, 337, 345, 363, 486), Metroline (4, 16, 32, 91, 113, 139, 186, 189, 204, 210, 263, 297, 332, 605, 606), Quality Line (406, 418, 467), Stagecoach (5, 53, 62, 99, 145, 174, 496)**

Enviro400 10.8m

Apart from Stagecoach's *Spirit of London* working out of West Ham, the only place to see 10.8 metre Enviro400s in the London area is on route 61. Ten have been based at Bromley since they were new.

Built: **Alexander Dennis**   Introduced: **2005 & 2006**   Number: **11**
Operators (routes): **Stagecoach (15, 61)**

Enviro400H 10.1m

London United has the greatest number of hybrid Enviro400s at twenty-two, until Metroline assumes that honour later in 2011. ADH8 runs along Regent Street on its usual route 94 work.

Built: **Alexander Dennis**   Introduced: **2008-2010**   Number: **42**
Operators (routes): **Go-Ahead (24), London United (94, 482), Metroline (16, 139, 189)**

Gemini 2 DL 10.4m

DW207, one of seventy-nine similar Wrightbus integrals based at Clapton garage, passes the eastern portico of Liverpool Street station.

Built: **Wrightbus**   Introduced: **2009-2011**   Number: **143**
Operators (routes): **Arriva (38, 59, 76, 123, 149, 242, 243), Arriva the Shires (640), First (23), Go-Ahead (88)**

Gemini 2 DL (E) 10.4m

The latest batch of Wrightbus integrals – DW401 onwards – have been built to the latest ECWVTA specification (see page 46). Barely a week after entering service, DW414 picks up passengers in Bishopsgate.

Built: **Wrightbus (to ECWVTA spec)**   Introduced: **2009-2011**   Number: **98**
Operators (routes): **Arriva (38, 59, 73, 76, 123, 149, 242, 243)**

Gemini 2 HEV 10.4m

Arriva has five of these and so does First. HW1 pulls out of London Bridge shortly before most of the bus station roof was demolished.

Built: **Wrightbus**   Introduced: **2008 & 2009**   Number: **10**
Operators (routes): **Arriva (141), FIrst (328)**

N94UD - OmniDekka 10.6m

London Sovereign's SLE25 in Harrow High Street. Twenty-two of these are based at the company's Edgware garage.

Built: **Scania/East Lancs**   Introduced: **2003-2006**   Number: **233**
Operators (routes): **Go-Ahead (425, 474), London Sovereign (13 114, 183, 292), London United (27, 267, 281), Metrobus (64, 119, 127, 161, 261, 320, 353, 405)**

N230UD - Olympus 10.8m

2007-built Olympus SEL742 at Marble Arch on route 7. Metroline operates thirty-three and the majority are based at Perivale.

Built: **Scania/East Lancs, Scania/Optare**   Introduced: **2007-2009**   Number: **63**
Operators (routes): **Metrobus (54, 75), Metroline (7, 90, 297)**

N230UD - OmniCity 10.8m

Metrobus's OmniCity 971 is about to leave its home garage at Beddington, Croydon, to work route 64.

Built: **Scania/East Lancs**   Introduced: **2008-2010**   Number: **420**
Operators (routes): **CT Plus (212), Go-Ahead (425), London Sovereign (13, 114, 183, 292), London United (10, 49, 57, 65, 111, 120, 131, 148, 267, 281, 371, 482, 697, H32, H91), Metrobus (64, 119, 320, 611), Stagecoach (48, 51, 53, 55, 56, 96, 106, 177, 205, 215, 248)**

Pulsar Gemini 2 HEV 10.4m

WHD1, the solitary example of its type, works route 24 alongside conventional and hybrid Enviro400s and a standard diesel Wrightbus, WDL1.

Built: **Wrightbus**   Introduced: **2008**   Number: **1**
Operators (routes): **Go-Ahead (24)**

Routemaster

Routemasters continue to pound London streets on two heritage routes, the 9 and the 15. First runs the former. The company's RM1627 waits between trips in Great Scotland Yard, close to Trafalgar Square.

Built: **AEC**   Introduced: **1959-1967**   Number: **19**
Operators (routes): **First (9), Stagecoach (15)**

Trident - ALX400 9.9m

Abellio's 9.9m ALX400 9829 heads along the Strand. This is one of fourteen of the type acquired from Metroline for the new contract to work route 172.

Built: **Dennis/Alexander, TransBus, Alexander Dennis**   Introduced: **1999-2005**   Number: **488**
Operators (routes): **Abelio (3, 157, 172, 211, 344, C3), London United (57, 65, 71, 111, 120, 131, 267, 281, 613, 671, 681, 691), Metroline (32, 266, 632, 643), Stagecoach (53, 115, 122, 136, 147, 175, 241, 247, 257, 262, 287, 294, 330, 473, 496, 541, 660, 678, 687)**

Trident - ALX400 10.5m

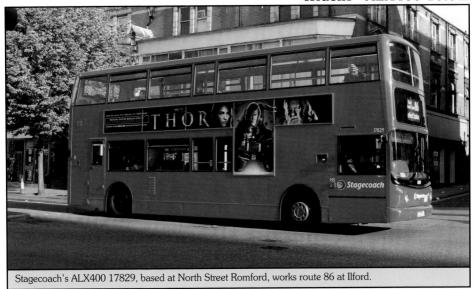

Stagecoach's ALX400 17829, based at North Street Romford, works route 86 at Ilford.

Built: **Dennis/Alexander, TransBus, Alexander Dennis** Introduced: **1999-2003/05/06** Number: **417**
Operators (routes): **First (23, 295, N26), London United (94, 220), Metroline (16, 32), Stagecoach (5, 8, 15, 26, 30, 47, 48, 53, 55, 56, 69, 86, 97, 99, 101, 103, 104, 115, 122, 136, 145, 158, 169, 199, 205, 208, 230, 238, 257, 269, 277, 287, 330, 387, 472, 601, 602, 608, 624, 625, 636, 637, 638, 647, 658, 664, 672, 678, 687)**

Trident - Lolyne 10.0m

CT Plus is the only London operator to use Trident Lolynes. The fleet of thirteen can usually be found on route 388. HTL13 waits at the stand in Whitehall Place.

Built: **TransBus/East Lancs** Introduced: **2003** Number: **10**
Operators (routes): **CT Plus** (388)

Trident (Enviro400) - Olympus 10.3m

Alexander Dennis provided the Enviro400 chassis for these Olympus-bodied double-deckers. Go-Ahead has fifty-three based at Sutton for routes 93, 154 & 213. The solitary DOE54, based at Merton, can often be found on route 77. In this shot, DOE39 coasts down the hill towards Wimbledon town centre.

Built: **Alexander Dennis/East Lancs, Alexander Dennis/Optare**   Introduced: **2008 & 2009**   Number: **55**
Operators (routes): **CT Plus (388, W13), Go-Ahead (93, 151, 154, 213)**

Trident - President 9.9m

A First-operated 9.9m President, TN33189, makes an unusual appearance on route 23 at Liverpool Street station. The TNA type, however, is quite common.

Built: **Dennis/Plaxton, TransBus**   Introduced: **1999-2003**   Number: **252**
Operators (routes): **CT Plus (388, 675), First (28, 67, 105, 282, 295, 357, 607, 616, U3, U4), Metroline (4, 16, 17, 134, 139, 140, 189, 217, 237, 263, 271, 603, 611, 626, 632, 635, 643, C2, W7, W8)**

Trident - President 10.5m

Metroline Presidents take a Sunday break from route 82 at Potters Bar garage. Left to right - TPL279, 251, 281, 277 & 284.

Built: **Dennis/Plaxton, TransBus**   Introduced: **2000-2002**   Number: **119**
Operators (routes): **First (179, 259, 476, 607, 652, 656, 679, 692, 699, D7), Metroline (4, 16, 43, 82, 134, 140, 182)**

The Garages

Bus garages in the London area come in all shapes, sizes and ages. Some are located on High Streets, others in anonymous industrial parks.

Some are traditional bus garages (i.e. built for buses) such as Sutton, others are former tram and trolleybus depots, like Holloway. This opened as a tram shed, but was then converted to a trolleybus depot before finally becoming a bus garage. Newer garages have been created inside industrial units, such as Beddington Cross They're not pretty and, frankly, they have no character, but they do the job.

The biggest garage in London (the biggest in Britain, for that matter) is the new West Ham, opened in 2008 with Capacity for more than 300 buses. On 17th September 2011, it swallowed up much of Upton Park's allocation too, when the long-standing garage by the football ground closed.

Each garage has a one- or two-letter code, used by London Buses for administrative purposes. Operators also give garages their own codes which, in most cases but not always, are the same as the ones assigned by London Buses. Within the book, we've used operators' codes exclusively, as these are the ones you're likely to see on the buses themselves. For the sake of completeness, where the code is different, it's shown in the following listing in parentheses underneath the operator's code.

The continued use of different coding systems from different eras means there is no uniformity. Many were created to a system introduced in the early part of the 20th Century by the London General Omnibus Company, which allocated codes alphabetically - A, B, C, etc., then AA, AB, AC, etc. So, Sutton became A and Camberwell was Q . . . which doesn't make a huge amount of sense. Later codes are a little more user-friendly, for example PM for **Peckham**.

Since the start of the tendering period in 1985, some codes have reflected the name of the owning company. BE, for instance, refers to Blue Triangle at Rainham. Some of these later additions have been retained as the building's code when the original operator has ceased to be – a system which, perversely, can also be traced back to the very earliest codes. As an example, the Tilling company had three garages at Bromley, Croydon and Lewisham which became TB, TC and TL. So far, so good, but it doesn't explain why TL is referred to as Catford in the modern world. Equally baffling at first sight is Abellio's garage at Battersea – QB – which actually stands for Q-Drive Battersea after the operator when the location was first used.

Some codes have been used for more than one garage over the years, or for different buildings in the same area. A new garage at Peckham, for instance, remained PM. There are other instances of codes lying dormant for many years before resurrection in a completely different area. Readers of a certain age will remember code C as Athol Street, Poplar . . . not Metrobus, Croydon.

Currently, three garages are shared by two companies in the same building and . . . yes, you've guessed . . . using different codes:

Edgware is both EW (the original code used by Metroline) and BT (used by London Sovereign).

Fulwell - FW (correct code used by London United) and TF (Abellio).

Ash Grove - AE (Arriva) and HK (CT Plus). This last one may be temporary as it's rumoured that HCT will be moving lock, stock and barrel to Walthamstow (WW in old money).

In conclusion, then, it's mad. Let us move on.

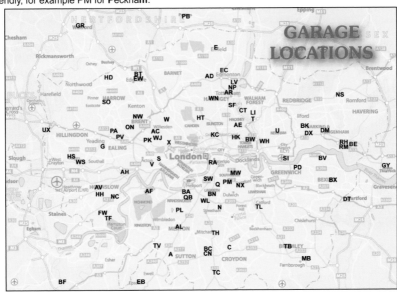

Five more of the Optare Olympus/Enviro400 combination inside their home garage at Sutton.

Code	Garage	Address/*Routes Operated*/Buses Allocated	PVR	Operator
A	Sutton	Bushey Road, Sutton, SM1 1QJ *80 93 151 154 164 213 413 N155* B7TL/Pres 10.0m, Dart/Est 10.4m, Dart/Point 10.1m, Env400, Tri/Olym 10.3m.	82	Go-Ahead
AC	Willesden	287 High Road, Willesden, London, NW10 2JY *6 52 98 260 302 460 N52 N98* B7TL/Pres 10.0m, B7TL/Pres 10.6m.	121	Metroline
AD	Palmers Green	Regents Avenue, London, N13 *102 125 329 629 634* DB250/Pres 10.6m, Env400.	56	Arriva
AE	Ash Grove	Mare Street, South Hackney, London, E8 *78 168 254 393* B7TL/Gem 10.1m, B7TL/Gem 10.6m, DB250/ALX400 10.5m, Dart/ALX200 10.2m, Dart/Point2 10.7m, Env400.	75	Arriva
AF	Putney	10 Chelverton Road, London, SW15 1RN *14 22 74 85 424 430 670 N22 N74* B7TL/Gem 10.1m, B9TL/Env400 10.4m, Dart/Point 8.8m.	112	Go-Ahead
AH	Brentford	Commerce Road, Brentford, Middlesex, TW8 8LZ *190 209 237 609 635 E2 E8* B9TL/Gem2, Dart/Evo 10.2m, Dart/Point 10.1m, Dart/Point2 10.1m, Env200 10.2m, OPTempH 10.6m, Tri/Pres 9.9m.	71	Metroline
AL	Merton	High Street, London, SW19 1DN *22 44 77 118 155 163 164 200 201 219 270 280 355 655 N155* B7TL/Gem 10.1m, B7TL/Pres 10.0m, Dart/Est 10.4m, Dart/Point 10.0m, Dart/Point 10.1m, Dart/Point2 10.1m, SB120/Cad 9.4m, Env200 10.2m, Env400, RM, Tri/Olym 10.3m.	162	Go-Ahead
AR	Tottenham	Philip Lane, High Cross, London, N15 *41 76 123 149 243 318 N41 N73 N76* B5LH/Gem2 10.4m, B7TL/ALX400 10.1m, Dart/Point2 8.8m, DB250/ALX400 10.2m, DB300/Gem2 10.4m.	133	Arriva

AV Hounslow
Kingsley Road, Hounslow
27 81 111 120 203 222 696 697 H32 H37 H98 N9   **132 London United**
B7TL/ALX400 10.1m, MBCit, CN94UD/Omni 10.7m,
Dart/Point 10.1m, Dart/Point2 10.1m, Dart/Point2 10.7m,
Env200 10.8m, N230UD/Omni 10.8m, OPTemp 12.0m.

BC Beddington
Unit 10, Beddington Cross, Beddington Farm Road, Croydon, CR0 4XH
3 152 157 322 407 434 931 N3 P13   **83 Abellio**
B7TL/Gem 10.6m, Dart/Point 8.8m, Dart/Point 10.1m,
Dart/Point2 10.1m, Dart/ALX200 8.9m, Env200 8.9m,
Env200 10.2m, Tri/ALX400 9.9m.

BE Rainham
Unit 3C, Denver Trading Estate, Ferry Lane, Rainham, Essex, RM13 9BU
167 347 362 364 649 650 651 674 EL1 EL2 W19   **55 Go-Ahead**
B7TL/Pres 10.0m, B7TL/Gem2 10.4m, Dart/Evo 10.8m,
Dart/Point 9.2m, Dart/Point 10.7m, Dart/Point2 10.7m, Env200 10.8m.

BK Barking
205 Longbridge Road, Barking, Essex, IG11 8UE
5 15 62 101 145 169 366 387 396 687 N15   **113 Stagecoach**
Dart/ALX200 10.2m, Dart/Point 10.1m, Env400, OPVer 10.4m,
Tri/ALX400 10.5m.

BN Brixton
39 Streatham Hill, London, SW2
19 59 137 159 319 N19   **135 Arriva**
B7TL/ALX400 10.1m, DB250/ALX400 10.2m, DB300/Gem2 10.4m

BT Edgware
Approach Road, Edgware, Middlesex, HA8 7AN
13 114 183 251 292 324 N13   **82 Lon. Sovereign**
B7TL/Pres 10.6m, B7TL/Vyk 11.0m, N94UD/Omni 10.6m,
N230UD/Omni 10.8m.

BV Belvedere
Burts Wharf, Crabtree Manorway North, Belvedere, DA17 6BT
180 244 669 N1   **27 Go-Ahead**
B7TL/Gem 10.6m, B7TL/Pres 10.0m, Env200 10.2m.

BW Bow
Fairfield Road, Bow, London, E3 2QP
8 15 205 277 N8   **106 Stagecoach**
N230UD/Omni 10.8m, RM, Tri/ALX400 9.9m, Tri/ALX400 10.5m.

An interesting assortment outside London Central's Bexleyheath garage. Both kinds of Enviro keep a Wrightbus Cadet and a Plaxton President company. The building was originally a trolleybus depot - the only one in the London area built specifically for that purpose.

BX Bexleyheath	Erith Road, Bexleyheath, Kent, DA7 6BX *89 132 229 321 401 422 486 661 669 B11 B16 N21 N89* B7TL/Pres 10.0m, B9TL/Gem2 10.4m, Dart/Evo 10.8m, Dart/Point 10.1m, SB120/Cad 9.4m, SB120/Cad 10.8m, Env200 10.2m, Env400.	**109 Go-Ahead**
C Croydon	134 Beddington Lane, Beddington, CR9 4ND *64 75 119 127 130 202 293 359 405 612 N64 T32 T33 X26* 14.240/Env200 10.7m, 14.240/Evo 10.8m, Dart/Point 10.7m, Dart/Point2 10.7m, CN94UB/Omni 12.0m, N94UD/Lancs 10.6m, N230UD/Olym 10.8m, N230UB/Omni 12.0m, N230UD/Lancs 10.8m, N230UD/Omni 10.8m.	**115 Metrobus**
CN Beddington	Beddington Farm Road, Croydon, Surrey, CR0 *264 403 410 450 455 627* Dart/ALX200 9.4m, Dart/Point 9.3m, DB250/ALX400 10.6m, DB250/Gem 10.3m, SB120/Cad 9.4m, SB120/Cad 10.2m.	**62 Arriva**
CT Clapton	15 Bohemia Place, Mare Street, London, E8 *38 242 393 N38* B7TL/Gem 10.1m, Dart/Point 9.3m, DB300/Gem2 10.4m, Env200 9.3m, Env400.	**101 Arriva**
CY Crawley (MY)	Wheatstone Close, Manor Royal, Crawley, West Sussex, RH10 9UA *465* Env200 10.2m.	**5 Metrobus**
DM Dagenham (RN)	73 Chequers Lane, Dagenham, Essex, RM9 6QJ *165 179 193 252 365 368 498 608 646 648 652 656 679 686 953* B7TL/Gem 10.1m, B12T/EXCA, Dart/Cap 8.9m, Dart/Cap 9.3m, Dart/Cap 10.2m, Dart/Nim 10.5m, Env200 10.2m, Env400, OLY/Pal, Tri/Pres 9.9m, Tri/Pres 10.5m.	**84 First**

Arriva's Enfield garage in Ponders End. Three Mini Darts - PDL141, 145 & 144 – stand in the yard on a slack Sunday.

Code	Garage	Address/*Routes Operated*/Buses Allocated	PVR	Operator
DT	Dartford	Central Road, Dartford, Kent, DA1 *126 160 233 286 428 492 B12 B13 B15* Dart/Point2 10.7m, DB250/Gem, Env200 8.9m, Env200 10.2m, Env200 10.8m, Enviro400 10.1m, SB120/Cad 9.4m.	69	Arriva Southern Counties
DX	Barking	Ripple Road, Barking *128 135 150 173 275 325 462 667* B7TL/ALX400 10.1m, B7TL/Gem 10.1m, Dart/Point2 8.8m, Env200 10.2m, Env400.	79	Arriva
E	Enfield	Southbury Road, Ponders End, EN1 *121 279 307 313 317 327 349 377 491 N279* B7TL/Gem 10.1m, Dart/Point 8.8m, Dart/Point 9.3m, Dart/Point2 8.8m, DB250/ALX400 10.2m, DB250/ALX400 10.6m, DB250/Pres 10.2m, DB250/Pres 10.6m, Env200 10.2m, SB120/Cad 10.2m, SB120/Cad 10.8m.	106	Arriva
EB	Epsom	Blenheim Road, Epsom, Surrey, KT19 9AF *404 406 411 418 463 467 470 641 K5 S1 S3 S4* Dart/ALX200 8.9m, Dart/Lancs 9.0m, Dart/Nimb 10.2m, E200/Est 9.5m, E200/Lancs 9.0m, Env200 8.9m, Env400, MBCit, OPSolo 8.5m, OPSolo 8.8m, OPVer 11.1m.	57	Quality Line
EC	Edmonton	Unit 1E, Towpath Road, Stonehill Business Park, London E4 *20 29 34 379 382 397 444 657 N29 W14 W15 W16* CITG, Dart/ALX200 9.4m, Dart/ALX200 10.2m, Dart/Point 8.8m, Dart/Point 9.3m, DB250/ALX400 10.2m, DB250/ALX400 10.6m, SB120/Cad 10.2m.	124	Arriva
EW	Edgware	Approach Road, Edgware, Middlesex, HA8 7AN *107 113 186 204 240 605 606 N5 N16 N98* B7TL/Pres 10.6m, Env400.	69	Metroline
FW	Fulwell	Wellington Road, Fulwell, Middlesex, TW2 5NX *65 71 110 131 216 267 281 290 371 671 681 691* Dart/Point2 10.1m, Env200 10.2m, Env200H 10.2m, N94UD/Omni 10.6m, N230UD/Omni 10.8m. Tri/ALX400 9.9m, Tri/ALX400 10.5m.	128	London United

Metroline's Harrow Weald garage and some of its Presidents - VP625, 622, 606 & 626. The garage opened in 1930 and the roof was extended over the original forecourt two years later to increase covered capacity.

Code Garage	Address/*Routes Operated*/Buses Allocated	PVR	Operator
G Greenford	Council Depot, Greenford Road, Greenford		
	92 95 282 E1 E3 E5 E7 E9 E10	117	First
	B7TL/Gem 10.6m, Dart/Cap 10.2m, Env200 8.9m, Env200 10.2m,		
	Env400, Tri/Pres 9.9m, Tri/Pres 10.5m.		
GR Watford	934 St. Albans Road, Watford, Hertfordshire, WD2 6NN		
	142 258 268 288 303 305 340 640 642 H1 H2 H3 H18 H19	70	Arriva The
	Dart/Point 8.8m, Dart/Point 10.2m, DB250/ALX400 10.2m,		Shires
	DB250/Gem 10.3m, DB300/Gem2 10.4m, OPSolo 7.8m,		
	SB120/Cad 10.2m.		
GY Grays	Unit 7, Europa Park, London Road, Grays, Essex, RM20 4DB		
	66 256 346 370 375 499	38	Arriva Southern
	Env200 10.2m, Env200 10.8m, SB120/Cad 9.4m, SB120/Cad 10.2m.		Counties
HD Harrow	467 High Road, Harrow Weald, Middlesex, HA3 6EJ		
Weald	*140 182 H12 N16*	56	Metroline
	B7TL/Pres 10.0m, B7TL/Pres 10.6m, Tri/Pres 10.5m.		
HH Hounslow	Tamian Way, Hounslow, Middlesex, TW4 6BL		
(WK) Heath	*116 285 423 482 698 H22 H91*	69	London United
	CN94UD/Omni 10.7m, Dart/Point 10.1m, Dart/Point2 10.1m,		
	Env200 10.2m, Env200 10.8m, N230UD/Omni 10.8m, Env400H.		
HK Ash Grove	Mare Street, South Hackney, London, E8		
	153 212 385 388 394 675 W5 W12 W13	63	CT Plus
	Dart/Comp 10.7m, Dart/Nim 8.9m, Dart/Nim 10.5m,		
	Dart/Point 8.8m, Dart/Point 9.2m, E200/Est 9.4m, Env200 8.9m,		
	N230UD/Omni 10.8m, OPSolo 7.8m, OPSolo 8.8m,		
	Tri/Loyl 10.0m, Tri/Olym 10.3m, Tri/Pres 9.9m.		
HS Hayes	Swallowfield Way, Hayes		
(HZ)	*195 207 427 N207*	62	First
	B9TL/Gem2 10.4m, CITG, Dart/Cap 8.9m, Dart/Cap 9.3m,		
	Dart/Cap 10.2m, Env200 10.2m.		
HT Holloway	37A Pemberton Gardens, London, N19 5RR		
	4 17 43 91 134 271 390 603 C2 N5 N20 N91 W7	185	Metroline
	B7TL/Pres 10.6m, Env400, Tri/Pres 9.9m, Tri/Pres 10.5m.		
KC King's	Freight Lane, London N1		
Cross	*46 214 274*	52	Metroline
	Dart/Point2 10.1m.		
LI Lea	151 Ruckholt Road, Leyton, London, E10 5PB		
(HO) Interchange	*25 26 30 58 236 308 309 339 686 N26 RV1 W11*	165	First
	B9TL/Gem2 10.4m, Dart/Cap 9.3m, Dart/Cap 10.2m,		
	Dart/Nim 10.5m, Env200 9.3m, Env200 10.2m, Env400,		
	Puls2Hydro, Tri/Pres 10.5m.		
LV Leeside	Leeside Road, Tottenham, N17		
Road	*192 341 628 653 683 688 W6*	52	Arriva
	Dart/Point 8.8m, Dart/Point 9.3m, Dart/Point2 8.8m, DB250/ALX400,		
	DB250/Pres, Env400.		
MB Orpington	Oak Farm, Farnborough Hill, Green Street Green, Orpington, Kent, BR6 6DA		
	54 75 138 146 161 162 181 261 284 320 336 352 353 358 367 464		
	654 B14 R1 R2 R3 R4 R5 R6 R7 R8 R9 R10 R11	171	Metrobus
	12.240/Lancs 10.3m, Dart/Cap 8.9m, Dart/Cap 10.2m,		
	Dart/Est 9.0m, Dart/Point 8.8m, Dart/Point 8.9m, Dart/Point2 8.8m,		
	Env200 8.9m, CN94UB/Omni 12.0m, N94UB/Est 10.6m,		
	N94UD/Lancs 10.6m, N230UD/Olym 10.8m, N230UD/Omni 10.8m.		
MW Mandela	Mandela Way, SE1 5SS		
Way East	*1 453 507 521 N1*	45	Go-Ahead
	B7TL/Gem 10.6m, CITG.		
N Norwood	Knights Hill, London, SE27		
	2 133 176 249 415 417 432 690 N2 N137	120	Arriva
	B7TL/ALX400 10.1m, B7TL/ALX400 10.6m, DB250/ALX400 10.2m,		
	Env400, RM.		
NC Twickenham	Twickenham Trading Estate, Rugby Road, Twickenham, Middlesex, TW1 1DU		
	33 419 493	42	London United
	Dart/Point 10.1m, Dart/Point2 10.1m, Env200 10.2m.		

Code	Garage	Address/*Routes Operated*/Buses Allocated	PVR	Operator
NP	Northumberland Park	Marsh Lane, Tottenham, London, N17 *67 191 231 259 299 357 389 399 476 616 692 699 W4 W10* B7TL/Pres 10.6m, B9TL/Gem2 10.4m, Dart/Cap 9.3m, Env200 8.9m, Env400, Tri/Pres 9.9m, Tri/Pres 10.5m.	108	First
NS	Romford	North Street, Romford, Essex, RM1 1DS *86 103 175 247 294 296 496 608 647 N86* Dart/ALX200 10.2m, Env200 10.2m, Env400, Tri/ALX400 9.9m, Tri/ALX400 10.5m.	92	Stagecoach
NX	New Cross	208 New Cross Road, London, SE14 *21 36 108 129 225 321 436 621 N21* B7TL/Pres 10.0m, B9TL/Gem2 10.4m, CITG, Dart/Evo 10.8m, Dart/Point 10.1m, Dart/Point 10.7m, 10.0m, Dart/Point2 10.1m, Env400, SB120/Cad 10.8m, RM.	116	Go-Ahead
ON	Alperton	Ealing Road, Alperton, Middlesex, HA0 *79 83 223 224 245* B7TL/Gem 10.1m, B9TL/Gem2 10.4m, Dart/Cap 9.3m, Dart/Cap 10.2m, Env200 10.2m, Tri/Pres 9.9m.	76	First
PA	Perivale (West)	Unit 12, Perivale IndusTrial Park, Horsenden Lane Sth, Greenford, UB6 7RL *105 143 297 326 395 C11 E6* Env200 10.2m, Env400, N230UD/Olym 10.8m.	96	Metroline
PB	Potters Bar	High Street, Potters Bar, Herts, EN6 5BE *82 84 217 234 263 383 384 626 N20 N91 W8 W9* Dart/Point 9.3m, Dart/Point2 8.8m, Dart/Point2 10.1m, Env200 8.9m, Env200 10.8m, Env400, Tri/Pres 9.9m, Tri/Pres 10.5m.	108	Metroline
PD	Plumstead	Pettman Crescent, Plumstead, London, SE28 0BJ *51 53 96 99 122 177 291 386 469 472 601 602 625 672* Dart/Point 9.3m, Dart/Point2 9.3m, Env200 9.3m, Env400, N230UD/Omni 10.8m, OPVer 10.4m, Tri/ALX400 9.9m, Tri/ALX400 10.5m.	163	Stagecoach

Potters Bar garage also opened in 1930. Enviro400 TE940 shares space with Enviro200s DEL849 & 857.

Code	Garage	Address/*Routes Operated*/Buses Allocated	PVR	Operator
PK	Park Royal	Atlas Road, Harlesden, London, NW10 6DN *272 283 440 C1 E11* Dart/Point2 10.1m, Env200 8.9m, Env200 10.2m, OPVer 10.4m.	53	London United
PL	Waterside Way	Waterside Way, London, SW17 0HB *39 485 G1* Dart/Point 8.8m, Dart/Point 10.1m, Dart/Point2 8.8m, Dart/Point2 9.3m, RM.	27	Go-Ahead
PM	Peckham	Blackpool Road, Peckham, London, SE15 3SE *36 37 63 363 N63 P12 X68* B7TL/Pres 10.0m, B9TL/Gem2 10.4m, 10.0m, Dart/Point2 9.3m, Env400.	70	Go-Ahead
PV	Perivale (East)	Alperton Lane, WEstern Avenue, Greenford, Middlesex, UB6 8DW *7 70 90 206 232 297 611 N7* 12.240/Evo 10.4m, Dart/Point 10.1m, Dart/Point2 10.1m, N230UD/Olym 10.8m.	75	Metroline
Q	Camberwell	1 Warner Road, Camberwell, London, SE5 9LU *12 42 45 68 171 185 360 468 N68 N171 P5 X68* B7TL/Gem 10.1m, B7TL/Gem 10.6m, B7TL/Pres 10.0m, CITG, Dart/Point 9.2m, Dart/Point 10.0m, Dart/Point2 9.3m, Dart/Point2 10.1m, Electy 10.3m, Electy 10.4m, Env200 9.3m, N94UB/Lanc 10.6m.	186	Go-Ahead
QB	Battersea	Silverthorne Road, Battersea, London, SW8 3HE *35 156 211 344 414 452 C3 C10 N3 N35* Env200 10.2m, Env400, Tri/ALX400 9.9m.	139	Abellio
RA	Waterloo	Cornwall Road, London, SE1 8TE *507 521* MBCit.	40	Go-Ahead
RM	Rainham	Unit 2, Albright IndusTrial Estate, Ferry Lane, Rainham, Essex, RM13 9BU *174 248 287 372* Env200 10.2m, Env200 10.8m, Env400, N230UD/Omni 10.8m, Tri/ALX400 9.9m, Tri/ALX400 10.5m.	47	Stagecoach
S	Shepherd's Bush	Wells Road, London, W12 *49 72 94 148 220 N97* B7TL/ALX400 10.1m, B7TL/Gem 10.1m, B7TL/Vyk 10.4m, Dart/Point2 10.1m, Env200 10.2m, Env400H, N230UD/Omni 10.8m, Tri/ALX400 10.5m.	113	London United

Among other locations, London United operates from the 1906-built Shepherds Bush garage. Most days reveal an interesting line-up, on this occasion OmniCity SP131, ALX400 TLA11 and Myllennium Vyking VE5.

SF	Stamford Hill	Rookwood Road, London N16 *73 253 N73 N253* B5TL/Gem, B7TL/Gem 10.1m, B7TL/Gem 10.6m, DB250/ALX400 10.6m.	88 Arriva
SI	Silvertown	Factory Road, Silvertown, London, E16 *276 300 425 474 549 673 D6 D7 D8 N551* B7TL/Pres 10.0m, B9TL/Gem2 10.4m, Dart/Evo 9.2m, Dart/Evo 10.4m, Dart/Point2 9.3m, Dart/Point2 10.1m, Env200 10.2m, Env200 10.8m, N94UD/Omni 10.6m, N230UD/Omni 10.8m, OPSolo 8.8m.	90 Go-Ahead
SO	Harrow	331 Pinner Road, Harrow *398 H9 H10 H11 H13 H14 H17* Dart/Point2 10.1m, Env200 8.9m, Env200 10.2m.	42 Lon. Sovereign
SW	Stockwell	Binfield Road, London, SW4 6ST *11 24 87 88 170 196 315 333 337 345 N11 N44 N87 639 670* B7TL/Gem 10.1m, B7TL/Pres 10.0m, B7TL/Vyk 10.4m, Dart/Point 8.8m, Dart/Point 10.7m, Dart/Point2 10.1m, Env200 10.8m, Env400, Env400H, GemHEV 10.4m, Gem2DL 10.4m.	185 Go-Ahead
T	Leyton	High Road, Leyton, London, E10 6AD *48 55 56 97 215 230 N55* N230UD/Omni 10.8m, Tri/ALX400 9.9m, Tri/ALX400 10.5m.	100 Stagecoach

The graceful arched roof of the 1952-built Stockwell garage soars above RML2604, Enviros E125 & 113, Presidents PVL192, 235 & 189, and a damaged Wrightbus Eclipse Gemini.

An Enviro200, 36315, waits for its next job inside Bromley garage. The building dates from 1924, but a yard has been added on spare land on the other side of the road.

Code Garage	Address/*Routes Operated*/Buses Allocated	PVR Operator
TB Bromley	111 Hastings Road, Bromley, Kent, BR2 8NH *61 208 227 246 269 314 354 636 637 638 664* Dart/ALX200 8.9m, Dart/ALX200 10.2m, Dart/ALX200 10.8m, Dart/Point 10.1m, Dart/Point2 11.3m, Env200 8.9m, Env200 10.8m, Env400 10.8m, Tri/ALX400 9.9m, Tri/ALX400 10.5m.	82 Stagecoach
TC Croydon	Brighton Road, Croydon, CR2 6EL *50 60 166 194 197 312 412 466 685 N133 T31* Dart/Point 10.1m, DB250/ALX400 10.2m, DB250/Gem 10.3m, Env200 10.2m, Env400.	108 Arriva

Also built by Tilling, in 1915, the South Croydon garage was heavily damaged by a bomb during World War II. The repaired building eventually re-opened in the mid-1950s and is now in the domain of Arriva London South.

TF	**Fulwell**	The Old Tram Depot, Stanley Road, Twickenham, Middlesex, TW2 5NP	
		117 235 481 490 941 969 H20 H25 H26 R68 R70	**80 Abellio**
		Dart/Point 8.8m, Dart/Point 10.1m, Dart/Point2 10.1m,	
		Dart/Nimb 10.5m, Dart/Point2 10.7m, Dart/Nimb 11m,	
		Dart/ALX200 8.9m, Env200 8.9m, Env200 10.2m, Tri/ALX400 9.9m.	
TH	**Thornton Heath**	719 London Road, Thornton Heath	
		109 198 250 255 289 N109	**78 Arriva**
		Dart/Point2 10.7m, DB250/ALX400 10.2m, DB250/ALX400 10.6m,	
		Env400, SB120/Cad 10.2m.	
TL	**Catford**	180 Bromley Road, Catford, London, SE6 2XA	
		47 124 136 178 199 273 356 380 624 658 660 N47 N136 P4	**100 Stagecoach**
		Dart/ALX200 8.9m, Dart/Point 8.8m, Dart/Point 9.3m,	
		Dart/Point 10.1m, Env200 8.9m, Tri/ALX400 9.9m, Tri/ALX400 10.5m.	
TV	**Tolworth**	Kingston Road, Tolworth	
		57 265 613 665 965 K1 K2 K3 K4	**73 London United**
		Dart/Point 8.8m, Dart/Point2 8.8m, Dart/Point2 10.1m,	
		Env200 8.9m, Tri/ALX400 9.9m.	
UX	**Uxbridge**	Bakers Road, Uxbridge	
		331 607 A10 N207 U1 U2 U3 U4 U5 U10	**86 First**
		Dart/Nim 10.5m, Env200 10.2m, Tri/Pres 9.9m, Tri/Pres 10.5m.	
V	**Stamford Brook**	72-74 Chiswick High Road, London, W4	
		9 10 27 391	**91 London United**
		11.190/VEC, B7TL/Gem 10.1m, B7TL/Vyk 11.0m,	
		CN94UD/Omni 10.7m, Dart/Point2 10.7m, N94UD/Omni 10.6m,	
		OPVer 10.4m.	
W	**Cricklewood**	329 Edgware Road, Dollis Hill, London, NW2 6JP	
		16 32 139 189 210 251 266 316 332 632 643	**168 Metroline**
		Dart/Point2 10.1m, Env200 10.2m, Env400, Env400H,	
		Tri/ALX400 9.9m, Tri/ALX400 10.5m, Tri/Pres 10.5m.	
WB (HI)	**High Wycombe**	Lincoln Road, Cressex Business Park, High Wycombe, HP12 3RH	
		U9	**3 Arriva The Shires**
		Dart/Point 8.8m.	
WH	**West Ham**	Stephenson Street, Canning Town, London, E16 4SA	
		5 69 104 106 115 147 158 238 241 257 262 323	
		330 473 488 541 678 D3 N15 N550	**202 Stagecoach**
		Dart/ALX200 8.9m, Dart/ALX200 10.2m, Dart/ALX200 10.8m,	
		Dart/Point 8.8m, Dart/Point 9.3m Env200 10.2m, Env400 10.8m,	
		N230UD/Omni 10.8m, OPTempH 10.6m, Tri/ALX400 9.9m,	
		Tri/ALX400 10.5m.	
WJ	**Willesden Junction**	Station Road, Harlesden, NW10	
		18 187 226 228 487 N18 PR2	**103 First**
		B9TL/Gem2 10.4m, Dart/Cap 9.3m, Dart/Cap 10.2m,	
		Env200 10.2m.	
WL	**Walworth**	301 Camberwell New Road, London, SE5 0TF	
		40 100 172 188 343 381 484 N343 N381	**122 Abellio**
		B7TL/Gem 10.6m, Dart/Point2 9.3m, Dart/Point2 10.1m,	
		ELEC 10.3m, Env 200 9.3m, Env400, Env400H, Tri/ALX400 9.9m.	
WN	**Wood Green**	Jolly Butchers Hill, High Road, London, N22	
		141 144 184 221 243 298 W3 617	**106 Arriva**
		B7TL/Gem 10.1m, DB250/ALX400 10.2m, DB250/ALX400 10.6m,	
		Env200 10.2m, Gem2HEV 10.4m, SB120/Cad 10.2m.	
WS	**Hayes**	West London Coach Centre, North Hyde Gardens, Hayes, UB3 4QT	
		112 350 H28 U7	**28 Abellio**
		B7TL/Gem 10.6m, Dart/Point2 8.8m, Dart/SPRY 10.3m,	
		Dart/Nimb 10.5m, Env200 10.2m	
X	**Westbourne Park**	Great Western Road, London, W9	
		9 23 28 31 295 328 N28 N31	**128 First**
		B7TL/Gem 10.1m, B7TL/Gem 10.6m, Env400, Tri/ALX400 10.5m,	
		Tri/Pres 9.9m, Gem2DL 10.4m, Gem2HEV 10.4m, RM.	

The Routes

It goes without saying that London has a wonderful variety of bus routes . . . and the capital boasts the best night-time service of any city in the world! As well as the night changeovers to N numbers (e.g. 35 to N35), other routes run 24 hours anyway and retain their usual identity (e.g. 24).

Each route has its own Peak Vehicle Requirement based on service frequency, length and passenger numbers. Route 38, for instance, runs from Clapton to Victoria at 3 minute intervals in the rush hour and has the highest PVR of 70 (all Wrightbus Gemini integrals). The longest routes are X26 from Heathrow to Croydon and N89 from Erith to Charing Cross - both 21 miles. As a general rule, routes running through Central London have higher PVRs.

The following pages take each route in turn and show details of requirements, frequency (M-S & Sun), operator, buses used and the garages they run from.

With roughly a fifth of London routes up for tender each year, there are bound to be numerous changes. This section is correct to 17th September 2011, but as companies helpfully announce changeovers in advance, we've also included details of known alterations in the coming months. New operators are shown where applicable. Some routes receiving new buses will retain their current operator.

There will also be temporary changes caused by roadworks diversions which, in some cases, can also mean a change of frequency and an adjustment to the PVR.

As the first edition of this book goes to press, it seems likely that the remaining bendybuses will be consigned to history by the end of 2011. The surviving routes - 12, 29, 436 & 453 – are due for conversion in November, with the last, Route 207, possibly brought forward to December from the original date of April 2012. So, catch them while you can.

Route	Start Date	Change
3	11 Feb 12	new Env400Hs
12	5 Nov 11	new Env400Hs
19	31 Mar 12	Go-Ahead - new double deckers
20	24 Mar 12	Go-Ahead - new double deckers
29	26 Nov 11	new Gemini 2 integrals
46	1 May 12	new Single deckers
61	3 Dec 11	existing & new Enviro400s
79	26 Nov 11	Metroline - new Gemini 2s
89	28 Jan 12	new Gemini 2s
101	3 Mar 12	PV to 12 - new Enviro400s
104	3 Mar 12	PV to 15 - exist & new Env400s
144	15 Oct 11	new Enviro400s
152	3 Dec 11	exististing & new Enviro200s
158	3 Mar 12	existing & new Enviro400s
160	1 Dec 11	new Enviro400s
206	28 Apr 12	First - new single-deckers

Route	Start Date	Change
207	7 Apr 12*	new OmniCitys
223	15 Oct 11	new single-deckers
224	15 Oct 11	new single-deckers
238	3 Mar 12	PV to 11 - new Enviro400s
249	31 Mar 12	Go-Ahead - new double deckers
266	19 May 12	First - new double-deckers
275	3 Mar 12	Stagecoach - new Enviro400s
279	15 Oct 11	new Enviro400s
290	1 Oct 11	Abellio - existing single deckers
297	1 Jan 12	new B9TL/Gemini 2s
298	4 Feb 12	Sullivans - new Enviro200s
308	3 Mar 12	new Enviro200s
309	3 Mar 12	CT Plus - new single deckers
313	5 Nov 11	new Enviro200s & one Enviro400
349	1 Nov 11	new Enviro400s
357	3 Mar 12	new double-deckers
379	10 Mar 12	new single-deckers
397	25 Feb 12	new single-deckers
413	3 Dec 11	new Enviro200s
436	19 Nov 11	new Enviro400 & 400H
453	19 Nov 11	new Enviro400s & B5L/Gemini 2 Hyb
455	3 Mar 12	Abellio - existing double-deckers
462	24 Mar 12	Go-Ahead - new-single deckers
493	31 Mar 12	Go-Ahead - new-single deckers
617	31 Mar 12	new double-decker
624	31 Dec 11	Go-Ahead - existing double-deckers
625	31 Dec 11	Go-Ahead - existing double-deckers
629	31 Mar 12	new double-decker
647	31 Mar 12	Arriva - existing double-deckers
658	31 Dec 11	Go-Ahead - new B9TL/Gemini 2s
667	31 Mar 12	First - existing double-deckers
678	31 Mar 12	Arriva - existing double-deckers
C2	28 Apr 12	Abellio - new double-deckers
N19	31 Mar 12	Go-Ahead - existing double-deckers
N29	26 Nov 11	new Gemini 2 Integrals
N207	7 Apr 12*	new OmniCity double-deckers
P12	8 Oct 11	new Enviro200s
PR2	15 Oct 11	Route Discontinued
R1	3 Dec 11	new Enviro200s
R4	3 Dec 11	existing & new Enviro200s
R11	3 Dec 11	new Enviro200s
U9	31 Dec 11	Abellio - existing single-deckers
W3	15 Oct 11	new Enviro400s
W11	3 Mar 12	Arriva - new single-deckers
W13	10 Mar 12	CT Plus - existing double-deckers
W14	25 Feb 12	First - new single-deckers
W15	3 Mar 12	First - new single-deckers
W16	3 Mar 12	First - new single-deckers

* possibly to be brought forward to December '11

No.	Route	PVR	Freq		Operator	Garage	Type Used
1	Canada Water - Tottenham Court Road Station	16	8	12	Go-Ahead	MW	B7TL/Gem
2	West Norwood - Marylebone Station	24	8	10	Arriva	N	B7TL/ALX400
3	Crystal Palace - Oxford Circus	22	8	12	Abellio	BC	Tri/ALX400
4	Archway - Waterloo	18	10	15	Metroline	HT	B7TL/Pres
							Env400
							Tri/Pres
5	Romford - Canning Town	29	7	8	Stagecoach	BK	Env400
							Tri/ALX400
6	Willesden Garage - Aldwych	26	6	10	Metroline	AC	B7TL/Pres
7	East Acton - Russell Square	23	8	12	Metroline	PV	N230/Olym
8	Bow - Oxford Circus	29	7	10	Stagecoach	BW	Tri/ALX400
9	Hammersmith - Aldwych	22	6	10	London United	V	B7TL/Vyk
	(Heritage service Kensington H.S. & Trafalgar Sq.)	5	20	20	First	X	RM
10	Hammersmith - King's Cross	25	8	12	London United	V	N230/Omni
11	Fulham - Liverpool Street	24	8	10	Go-Ahead	SW	B7TL/Gem
12	Dulwich Library - Oxford Circus	31	5	6	Go-Ahead	Q	Citartic
13	Golders Green - Aldwych	20	8	12	Lon. Sovereign	BT	N94/Omni
							N230/Omni
							B7TL/Pres
							B7TL/Vyk
14	Putney Heath - University College Hospital	34	6	10	Go-Ahead	AF	B7TL/Gem

Routes 9 & 15 are supplemented by a heritage service operated with Routemasters between 09.30 and 18.30. RM1933 approaches the Tower Hill stop where it will begin its journey to Trafalgar Square.

15	Blackwall Station - Piccadilly Circus	24	8	8	Stagecoach	BW	Tri/ALX400
	(Heritage service between Tower Hill & Trafalgar Sq.)	5	15	15	Stagecoach	BW	RM
16	Cricklewood - Victoria	22	6	10	Metroline	W	Env400
							Env400H
							Tri/ALX400
							Tri/Pres

No.	Route	PVR	Freq		Operator	Garage	Type Used
17	Archway - London Bridge	16	8	15	Metroline	HT	B7TL/Pres Tri/Pres
18	Sudbury - Euston	48	4	7	First	WJ	B9TL/Gem2
19	Battersea Bridge - Finsbury Park	28	8	10	Arriva	BN	DB250/Gem
20	Debden - Walthamstow	9	15	30	Arriva	EC	DB250/ALX400

Route 21 is operated by Go-Ahead's New Cross garage, mostly with nearly-new Volvo-powered Eclipse Gemini 2s but also the odd President. From the 2011 delivery, WVL386 passes the forbidding exterior of the Bank of England.

No.	Route	PVR	Freq		Operator	Garage	Type Used
21	Lewisham - Newington Green	25	7	12	Go-Ahead	NX	B7TL/Pres B9TL/Gem2
22	Putney Common - Piccadilly Circus	22	8	12	Go-Ahead	AF	B7TL/Gem2
23	Westbourne Park - Liverpool Street	31	7	10	First	X	Tri/ALX400 Env400 Gem2
24	Hampstead Heath - Pimlico	29	5	8	Go-Ahead	SW	Env400 Env400H GemHEV
25	Ilford - Oxford Circus	59	4	6	First	LI	B9TL/Gem2
26	Hackney Wick - Waterloo	17	10	12	First	LI	Env400
27	Turnham Green - Camden Town	27	8	12	London United	V	B7TL/Vyk N94/Omni N230/Omni
28	Wandsworth - Kensal Rise	23	8	10	First	X	B7TL/Gem Tri/Pres
29	Wood Green Station - Trafalgar Square	29	6	6	Arriva	EC	Citartic
30	Hackney Wick - Marble Arch	23	10	12	First	LI	Env400
31	White City - Camden Town	24	6	6	First	X	B7TL/Gem

No.	Route	PVR	Freq		Operator	Garage	Type Used
32	Edgware - Kilburn	17	8	12	Metroline	W	Env400
							Tri/ALX400
							Tri/Pres
33	Fulwell - Hammersmith	18	8	15	London United	NC	Env200
34	Barnet - Walthamstow	20	9	12	Arriva	EC	DB250/ALX400
35	Clapham Junction - Shoreditch	19	10	15	Abellio	QB	Env400
36	New Cross Gate - Queens Park	27	6	12	Go-Ahead	NX	B7TL/Pres
							Env400
37	Putney Heath - Peckham	19	10	12	Go-Ahead	PM	B9TL/Gem2
							Env400

Route 38 has the highest PVR of any London route. Its allocation is based at Arriva's Clapton garage and entirely comprises Wrightbus integrals from the DW201 and DW401 batches. DW420, one of the newer buses built to the ECWVTA specification, begins its journey from Victoria station.

No.	Route	PVR	Freq		Operator	Garage	Type Used
38	Clapton - Victoria	70	4	5	Arriva	CT	DB300/Gem2
39	Putney - Clapham Junction	15	8	12	Go-Ahead	PL	Dar/Point
40	Dulwich Library - Aldgate	16	8	15	Abellio	WL	Env400
41	Tottenham Hale - Archway	21	5	10	Arriva	AR	B7TL/ALX400
							DB250/ALX400
42	Denmark Hill - Bishopsgate	11	10	15	Go-Ahead	Q	Omni/Myll
43	Friern Barnet - London Bridge	33	8	10	Metroline	HT	B7TL/Pres
							Tri/Pres
44	Tooting Station - Victoria	16	10	15	Go-Ahead	AL	B7TL/Gem
							B7TL/Pres
45	Clapham Park - King's Cross	22	8	15	Go-Ahead	Q	B7TL/Gem
							B7TL/Pres
46	Lancaster Gate - Farringdon Street	17	10	15	Metroline	KC	Dar/Point
47	Bellingham Catford Bus Garage - Shoreditch	17	10	15	Stagecoach	TL	Tri/ALX400
48	Walthamstow - London Bridge	20	8	12	Stagecoach	T	N230/Omni
							Tri/ALX400

No.	Route	PVR	Freq		Operator	Garage	Type Used
49	Clapham Junction - White City	19	8	10	London United	S	B7TL/Vyk
50	Croydon - Stockwell	15	12	20	Arriva	TC	DB250/ALX400
							DB250/Gem
							Env400
51	Orpington - Woolwich	17	10	15	Stagecoach	PD	N230/Omni
52	Willesden - Victoria	25	6	8	Metroline	AC	B7TL/Pres
53	Plumstead Station - Whitehall	27	8	10	Stagecoach	PD	Env400
54	Elmers End Station - Woolwich	14	14	15	Metrobus	MB	N230/Olym
55	Leyton Green - Oxford Circus	29	7	10	Stagecoach	T	N230/Omni
							Tri/ALX400
56	Whipps Cross - Smithfield	21	7	8	Stagecoach	T	N230/Omni
							Tri/ALX400
57	Kingston - Clapham Park	26	8	12	London United	TV	Tri/ALX400
58	East Ham - Walthamstow	15	10	15	First	LI	B9TL/Gem2

The Wrightbus integrals based at Brixton garage appear with other types on route 59. DW287 is closely pursued in Brixton High Street by DW293.

No.	Route	PVR	Freq		Operator	Garage	Type Used
59	Streatham Hill - King's Cross	23	7	12	Arriva	BN	DB250/ALX400
							DB250/Gem
							DB300/Gem2
60	Old Coulsdon - Streatham Common	16	12	20	Arriva	TC	DB250/ALX400
							DB250/Gem
61	Chislehurst Gordon Arms - Bromley	11	15	20	Stagecoach	TB	Env400
62	Marks Gate - Gascoigne Estate	15	10	20	Stagecoach	BK	Env200
							Env400
63	Honor Oak - King's Cross	27	6	8	Go-Ahead	PM	B7TL/Pres
							B9TL/Gem2
							Env400
64	New Addington - Thornton Heath Bus Garage	14	8	15	Metrobus	C	N94/Omni
							N230/Omni
65	Kingston - Ealing	21	8	10	London United	FW	N230/Omni
							Tri/ALX400

No.	Route	PVR	Freq		Operator	Garage	Type Used
66	Romford - Leytonstone	11	12	30	Arriva Sth Cou.	GY	Env200
67	Wood Green Station - Aldgate	15	10	12	First	NP	B7TL/Pres
							Tri/Pres
68	West Norwood - Euston	21	8	12	Go-Ahead	Q	B7TL/Gem
							B7TL/Pres
69	Walthamstow - Canning Town	18	8	12	Stagecoach	WH	Tri/ALX400
70	Acton - South Kensington	15	10	15	Metroline	PV	Dar/Point
71	Chessington World of Adventures - Kingston	12	8	12	London United	FW	N230/Omni
							Tri/ALX400
72	Roehampton - East Acton	16	8	12	London United	S	Env200
73	Seven Sisters - Victoria	51	4	6	Arriva	SF	Gem2INT
							B5L/Gem2
74	Putney - Baker Street	21	8	10	Go-Ahead	AF	B7TL/Gem
75	Croydon - Lewisham	13	14	15	Metrobus	C	N230/Olym
76	Tottenham - Waterloo	22	8	12	Arriva	AR	B5L/Gem2
							DB250/ALX400
							DB300/Gem2
77	Tooting Station - Waterloo	16	10	12	Go-Ahead	AL	B7TL/Gem
							B7TL/Pres
78	Nunhead - Shoreditch	16	9	12	Arriva	AE	Env400
79	Edgware - Alperton	11	13	15	First	ON	B7TL/Gem
							B9TL/Gem2
80	Belmont Highdown Prison - Hackbridge	10	12	20	Go-Ahead	A	E200/Est
							Dar/Point
81	Slough - Hounslow	13	12	20	London United	AV	B7TL/ALX400
							B7TL/Pres
							CN94/Omni
82	North Finchley - Victoria	24	9	13	Metroline	PB	Tri/Pres
83	Ealing Hospital - Golders Green	28	8	10	First	ON	B7TL/Gem
							B9TL/Gem2
85	Kingston - Putney	15	8	10	Go-Ahead	AF	B7TL/Gem
							B9TL/Env400
86	Romford - Stratford	28	6	10	Stagecoach	NS	Tri/ALX400
87	Wandsworth - Aldwych	21	6	12	Go-Ahead	SW	B7TL/Gem
							B7TL/Pres
88	Clapham Common - Camden Town	22	8	12	Go-Ahead	SW	B7TL/Gem
							B7TL/Pres
							Env400
89	Slade Green - Lewisham	15	10	20	Go-Ahead	BX	B7TL/Pres
							B9TL/Gem
90	Feltham - Northolt	17	10	20	Metroline	PV	Dar/Point
							Man240/Evo
							N230/Olym
91	Crouch End - Trafalgar Square	19	8	10	Metroline	HT	Env400
92	Brent Park - Ealing Hospital	18	8	10	First	G	B7TL/Gem
							Env400
93	North Cheam - Putney	21	7	10	Go-Ahead	A	B7TL/Pres
							Env400
							Tri/Olym
94	Acton Green - Piccadilly Circus	30	5	8	London United	S	Env400H
							Tri/ALX400
95	Southall - Shepherd's Bush	14	12	20	First	G	Env200
96	Bluewater - Woolwich	21	8	12	Stagecoach	PD	N230/Omni
97	Chingford - Leyton	14	10	15	Stagecoach	T	Tri/ALX400
98	Willesden - Holborn	25	6	8	Metroline	AC	B7TL/Pres
99	Bexleyheath - Woolwich	12	12	15	Stagecoach	PD	Env400
							Tri/ALX400
100	Shadwell - Elephant & Castle	18	8	12	Abellio	WL	Env200
101	Wanstead - Gallions Reach Shopping Park	11	12	15	Stagecoach	BK	Tri/ALX400

No.	Route	PVR	Freq		Operator	Garage	Type Used
102	Edmonton Green - Brent Cross	24	9	12	Arriva	AD	Env400
103	Chase Cross - Rainham	12	10	20	Stagecoach	NS	Tri/ALX400
104	Manor Park - Stratford	15	10	15	Stagecoach	WH	Tri/ALX400
105	Greenford Station - Heathrow Airport Central	16	10	15	Metroline	PA	B9TL/Gem2
106	Finsbury Park - Whitechapel	18	8	10	Stagecoach	WH	N230/Omni
107	New Barnet Station - Edgware	9	15	20	Metroline	EW	B7TL/Pres

New Cross-based DWL27, known as a Volvo Merit but in reality a VDL SB120/Wrightbus Cadet (!), pauses on the route 108 stand at the old Stratford bus station.

No.	Route	PVR	Freq		Operator	Garage	Type Used
108	Lewisham - Stratford	14	10	15	Go-Ahead	NX	Dar/Evo Dar/Point SB120/Cadet
109	Croydon - Brixton	25	6	10	Arriva	TH	DB250/ALX400 Env400
110	Twickenham - Hounslow	5	20	30	London United	FW	Dar/Point
111	Heathrow Airport Central - Kingston	23	10	12	London United	AV	B7TL/ALX400 N230/Omni Tri/ALX400
112	Ealing - Brent Cross	7	15	20	Abellio	WS	Dar/Nimb
113	Edgware - Marble Arch	18	10	20	Metroline	EW	B7TL/Pres Env400
114	Ruislip - Mill Hill	12	10	12	Lon. Sovereign	BT	B7TL/Pres B7TL/Vyk N94/Omni N230/Omni
115	East Ham - Aldgate	19	8	10	Stagecoach	WH	Tri/ALX400
116	Ashford Hospital - Hounslow	6	12	20	London United	HH	Dar/Point
117	Staines - Isleworth	9	20	30	Abellio	FW	Env200
118	Morden - Brixton	12	12	20	Go-Ahead	AL	B7TL/Gem B7TL/Pres Env400

No.	Route	PVR	Freq		Operator	Garage	Type Used
119	Bromley - Purley Way	16	10	15	Metrobus	C	N94/Omni
							N230/Omni
120	Northolt - Hounslow	16	10	12	London United	AV	B7TL/ALX400
							B7TL/Pres
							CN94/Omni
							N230/Omni
							Tri/ALX400
121	Enfield Lock - Turnpike Lane Station	20	11	15	Arriva	E	DB250/ALX400
122	Plumstead Bus Garage - Crystal Palace	16	12	15	Stagecoach	PD	Tri/ALX400

Old and new on the stands at Ilford: An Arriva ALX400 delivered in 2001, DLA298, is working route 123 while the EL2 benefits from a 2010-built Eclipse Gemini 2, WVL339. Sixteen of these newer Wrightbuses with Volvo B9 chassis are branded as East London Transit and allocated to Rainham, Ferry Lane, garage for routes EL1 & EL2.

No.	Route	PVR	Freq		Operator	Garage	Type Used
123	Ilford - Wood Green Station	19	10	15	Arriva	AR	B7TL/ALX400
							DB250/ALX400
							DB300/Gem2
124	Eltham - Catford	11	12	20	Stagecoach	TL	Dar/ALX200
							Dar/Point
125	Winchmore Hill - Finchley	12	10	15	Arriva	AD	DB250/Pres
126	Eltham - Bromley	10	11	20	Arriva Sth Cou.	DT	Dar/Point
127	Purley - Tooting	10	15	30	Metrobus	C	N94/Omni
128	Claybury - Romford	12	12	20	Arriva	DX	B7TL/ALX400
129	North Greenwich - Greenwich	4	12	20	Go-Ahead	NX	Dar/Evo
130	New Addington - Norwood Junction	8	15	30	Metrobus	C	Dar/Point
131	Kingston - Tooting	20	8	12	London United	FW	N230/Omni
							Tri/ALX400
132	Bexleyheath - North Greenwich	12	12	20	Go-Ahead	BX	SB120/Cadet
							Dar/Point
133	Streatham - Liverpool Street Station	30	7	12	Arriva	N	Env400
134	North Finchley - Tottenham Court Road	30	7	8	Metroline	HT	B7TL/Pres
							Tri/Pres
135	Crossharbour - Old Street Station	13	10	15	Arriva	DX	Env400
136	Grove Park - Peckham	13	10	12	Stagecoach	TL	Tri/ALX400
137	Streatham Hill - Marble Arch	27	6	8	Arriva	BN	DB300/Gem2
							DB250/Gem

No.	Route	PVR	Freq		Operator	Garage	Type Used
138	Coney Hall - Bromley	3	20	30	Metrobus	MB	Dar/Myll
139	West Hampstead - Waterloo	21	8	12	Metroline	W	Env400
							Env400H
							Tri/Pres
140	Harrow Weald - Heathrow Airport Central	22	8	12	Metroline	HD	B7TL/Pres
							Tri/Pres
141	Wood Green Station - London Bridge	23	7	12	Arriva	WN	B7TL/Gem
							DB250/ALX400
							Gem2 HEV
142	Watford - Brent Cross	15	12	15	Arriva Shires	GR	DB250/ALX400
143	Brent Cross - Archway	12	12	15	Metroline	PA	Env200
144	Edmonton Green - Muswell Hill	16	8	10	Arriva	WN	B7TL/Gem
							DB250/ALX400
							DB250/Pres
145	Dagenham - Leytonstone	15	12	20	Stagecoach	BK	Env400
							Tri/ALX400
146	Downe - Bromley	1	60	60	Metrobus	MB	Dar/Myll
147	Ilford - Canning Town Station	16	8	10	Stagecoach	WH	Tri/ALX400
148	Denmark Hill - White City	25	8	10	London United	S	B7TL/ALX400
							N230/Omni

A Shepherds Bush Scania OmniCity, SP118, passes two of London's most famous landmarks. Heavy traffic has caused this journey to be turned short at Victoria.

No.	Route	PVR	Freq		Operator	Garage	Type Used
149	Edmonton Green - London Bridge	36	8	8	Arriva	AR	B5L/Gem2 DB300/Gem2
150	Chigwell Row - Becontree Heath	12	12	20	Arriva	DX	Env400
151	Worcester Park - Wallington	13	10	20	Go-Ahead	A	B7TL/Pres Tri/Olym
152	New Malden - Pollards Hill	13	12	20	Abellio	BC	Dar/Point Env200
153	Finsbury Park - Liverpool Street	10	12	15	CT Plus	HK	Dar/Nimb
154	Morden - Croydon	12	12	20	Go-Ahead	A	B7TL/Pres Tri/ALX400 Tri/Olym
155	Tooting - Elephant & Castle	17	8	12	Go-Ahead	AL	B7TL/Gem B7TL/Pres
156	Wimbledon - Vauxhall	16	8	12	Abellio	QB	Env400
157	Morden - Crystal Palace	16	12	20	Abellio	BC	B7TL/Gem Tri/ALX400
158	Chingford Mount - Stratford	13	10	12	Stagecoach	WH	Tri/ALX400
159	Streatham - Paddington Basin	38	6	12	Arriva	BN	B7TL/ALX400 DB300/Gem2
160	Sidcup - Catford	11	15	20	Arriva Sth Cou.	DT	DB250/ALX400
161	Chislehurst - North Greenwich	14	10	12	Metrobus	MB	N94/Omni
162	Eltham Station - Beckenham Junction	8	20	30	Metrobus	MB	Env200
163	Morden - Wimbledon	12	8	12	Go-Ahead	AL	E200/Est
164	Sutton - Wimbledon	12	10	15	Go-Ahead	AL	Dar/Point E200/Est
165	Abbey Wood Lane - Romford Brewery	11	12	20	First	DM	Env200
166	Epsom General Hospital - Croydon	8	20	30	Arriva	TC	Dar/Point Env200
167	Debden - Ilford	9	20	30	Go-Ahead	BE	E200/Evo

Route 168 is worked by a mixture of Volvo B7/Eclipse Geminis and Enviro400s. One of each heads south on Eversholt Street in a classic example of 'bunching' – a regular occurrence in Greater London.

168	Hamspstead Heath - Old Kent Road	20	7	12	Arriva	AE	B7TL/Gem Env400
169	Clayhall - Barking	12	10	15	Stagecoach	BK	Env400

No.	Route	PVR	Freq		Operator	Garage	Type Used
170	Roehampton - Victoria	19	8	12	Go-Ahead	SW	Dar/Point Env200
171	Bellingham Catford Bus Garage - Holborn	24	8	12	Go-Ahead	NX	B7TL/Pres B9TL/Gem2
172	Brockley Rise - St. Paul's	15	10	15	Abellio	WL	Tri/ALX400
173	Little Heath King George Hospital - Beckton	11	12	20	Arriva	DX	Env200

Newly-delivered to Rainham garage, Enviro400 19729 stands at Dagnam Park in Harold Hill before returning to Dagenham.

No.	Route	PVR	Freq		Operator	Garage	Type Used
174	Harold Hill - Dagenham Marsh Way	20	8	15	Stagecoach	RM	Env400
175	Hillrise Estate - Dagenham Ford's Main Works	12	12	20	Stagecoach	NS	Tri/ALX400
176	Penge - Tottenham Court Road Station	25	8	12	Arriva	N	B7TL/ALX400 DB250/ALX400
177	Thamesmead - Peckham	18	10	12	Stagecoach	PD	N230/Omni
178	Woolwich - Lewisham	8	15	20	Stagecoach	TL	Dar/Point
179	Chingford - Ilford	10	12	20	First	DM	Env400
180	Thamesmead - Lewisham	14	12	20	Go-Ahead	BV	B7TL/Gem
181	Grove Park - Lewisham	11	12	15	Metrobus	MB	N94/Est
182	Harrow Weald - Brent Cross	22	8	12	Metroline	HD	B7TL/Pres Tri/Pres
183	Pinner - Golders Green	18	10	15	Lon. Sovereign	BT	B7TL/Pres B7TL/Vyk N94/Omni N230/Omni
184	Barnet - Turnpike Lane Station	17	10	12	Arriva	WN	Env200
185	Lewisham - Victoria	20	10	12	Go-Ahead	Q	B7TL/Gem B7TL/Pres
186	Northwick Park Hospital - Brent Cross	14	20	20	Metroline	EW	B7TL/Pres Env400
187	Central Middlesex Hospital - Finchley Road	14	10	15	First	WJ	Env200
188	North Greenwich - Russell Square	22	8	12	Abellio	WL	B7TL/Gem
189	Brent Cross - Oxford Circus	17	8	12	Metroline	W	Env400 Env400H Tri/Pres
190	Richmond - West Brompton	9	15	20	Metroline	AH	E200/Evo
191	Brimsdown - Edmonton Green	15	10	15	First	NP	Env400
192	Enfield - Edmonton Green	13	10	15	Arriva	LV	Env200
193	County Park Estate - Queen's Hospital	11	9	30	First	DM	Dar/Cap

No.	Route	PVR	Freq		Operator	Garage	Type Used
194	Croydon - Lower Sydenham	14	12	20	Arriva	TC	DB250/ALX400 DB250/Gem
195	Charville Lane - Brentford	14	12	15	First	HS	Env200
196	Norwood Junction - Elephant & Castle	14	12	20	Go-Ahead	SW	Env400
197	Croydon - Peckham	14	12	20	Arriva	TC	DB250/ALX400 Env400

DLA383 travels alongside the Tramlink at Sandilands on its way out of Croydon.

No.	Route	PVR	Freq		Operator	Garage	Type Used
198	Shrublands - Thornton Heath	12	10	20	Arriva	TH	DB250/ALX400 Env400
199	Bellingham Catford Bus Garage - Canada Water	10	12	15	Stagecoach	TL	Env400
200	Raynes Park - Mitcham	15	8	12	Go-Ahead	AL	Env200 E200/Est
201	Morden - Herne Hill	9	15	20	Go-Ahead	AL	Dar/Point SB120/Cadet
202	Blackheath - Crystal Palace	14	10	15	Metrobus	C	Man240/Evo
203	Staines - Hounslow	6	20	30	London United	AV	Citaro
204	Edgware - Sudbury	14	10	15	Metroline	EW	Env400
205	Bow - Paddington	26	8	12	Stagecoach	BW	N230/Omni Tri/ALX400
206	St. Raphael's Estate - Kilburn	8	15	20	Metroline	PV	Dar/Point Man240/Evo
207	Southall - White City	26	7	8	First	HS	Citartic
208	Orpington - Lewisham	15	12	15	Stagecoach	TB	Tri/ALX400
209	Mortlake - Hammersmith	14	6	10	Metroline	AH	Dar/ALX200 Dar/Point Env200
210	Brent Cross - Finsbury Park	16	8	10	Metroline	W	Env400
211	Hammersmith - Waterloo Station	18	8	12	Abellio	QB	Tri/ALX400
212	Chingford - Walthamstow	9	10	15	CT Plus	HK	N230/Omni
213	Sutton Bus Garage - Kingston	19	9	12	Go-Ahead	A	B7TL/Pres Env400 Tri/Olym

No.	Route	PVR	Freq		Operator	Garage	Type Used
214	Highgate - Liverpool Street Station	18	8	12	Metroline	KC	Dar/Point
215	Yardley Lane Estate - Walthamstow	4	20	30	Stagecoach	T	N230/Omni
216	Staines - Kingston	8	20	30	London United	FW	Dar/Point Env200
217	Waltham Cross - Turnpike Lane Station	11	12	20	Metroline	PB	Tri/Pres
219	Wimbledon - Clapham Junction	11	12	15	Go-Ahead	AL	Dar/Point E200/Est

One of the wonderfully noisy Volvo-powered ALX400s, VA90, runs the Shepherds Bush Green one-way circuit while heading for Wandsworth.

No.	Route	PVR	Freq		Operator	Garage	Type Used
220	Harlesden - Wandsworth	23	8	10	London United	S	B7TL/ALX400 Tri/ALX400
221	Edgware - Turnpike Lane Station	22	12	12	Arriva	WN	B7TL/Gem DB250/ALX400 DB250/Pres
222	Uxbridge - Hounslow	17	8	12	London United	AV	B7TL/ALX400 Dar/Point
223	Harrow - South Kenton - Wembley	6	20	30	First	ON	Dar/Cap
224	Wembley Stadium Station - Willesden Junc. Station	10	15	30	First	ON	Dar/Cap
225	Hither Green - Canada Water	7	15	20	Go-Ahead	NX	Dar/Point
226	Ealing - Golders Green	15	13	20	First	WJ	Env200
227	Bromley - Crystal Palace	13	8	12	Stagecoach	TB	Dar/Point
228	Park Royal - Maida Hill	12	12	20	First	WJ	Env200
229	Thamesmead - Sidcup	18	10	15	Go-Ahead	BX	B9TL/Gem2
230	Upper Walthamstow - Wood Green Station	12	12	15	Stagecoach	T	Tri/ALX400
231	Enfield - Turnpike Lane Station	6	15	20	First	NP	Env400
232	St. Raphael's Est - Turnpike Lane Station	11	20	20	Metroline	PV	Dar/Point Man240/Evo
233	Swanley - Eltham	6	20	30	Arriva Sth Cou.	DT	Env200
234	Barnet - East Finchley	12	12	20	Metroline	PB	Dar/Point
235	Lower Sunbury - Brentford	19	9	12	Abellio	TF	Dar/Nimb Dar/Point

First London's DML41422, a Dennis Dart with a Marshall Capital body, moves off from Homerton Hospital.

No.	Route	PVR	Freq		Operator	Garage	Type Used
236	Hackney Wick - Finsbury Park	15	8	12	First	LI	Dar/Cap
							Dar/Nimb
237	Hounslow Heath - White City	20	9	12	Metroline	AH	B9TL/Gem2
							Tri/Pres
238	Barking - Stratford	10	10	15	Stagecoach	WH	Tri/ALX400
240	Edgware - Golders Green	11	12	20	Metroline	EW	B7TL/Pres
241	Stratford - Canning Town	9	10	20	Stagecoach	WH	Tri/ALX400
242	Homerton Hospital - Tottenham Court Road	28	6	10	Arriva	CT	B7TL/Gem
							DB300/Gem2
							Env400
243	Wood Green Station - Waterloo	30	7	10	Arriva	AR	B5L/Gem2
							DB250/ALX400
							DB300/Gem2
244	Abbey Wood - Queen Elizabeth Hospital	12	10	15	Go-Ahead	BV	Env200
245	Alperton - Golders Green	21	8	12	First	ON	Env200
246	Westerham - Bromley	4	30	60	Stagecoach	TB	Env200
247	Barkingside - Romford	11	10	20	Stagecoach	NS	Tri/ALX400
248	Cranham - Romford	14	8	15	Stagecoach	RM	N230/Omni
249	Anerley Station - Clapham Common	12	12	15	Arriva	N	B7TL/ALX400
							DB250/ALX400
250	Croydon - Brixton	23	8	12	Arriva	TH	DB250/ALX400
							Env400
251	Edgware - Arnos Grove	12	12	20	Lon. Sovereign	BT	Env200
252	Collier Row - Hornchurch	12	10	15	First	DM	Env400
253	Hackney Central Station - Euston	27	6	8	Arriva	SF	B7TL/Gem
							DB250/ALX400
254	Holloway Parkhurst Road - Aldgate	29	6	8	Arriva	AE	B7TL/Gem
							DB250/ALX400

No.	Route	PVR	Freq		Operator	Garage	Type Used
255	Pollards Hill - Streatham Hill	8	12	20	Arriva	TH	Dar/Point
							SB120/Cadet
256	Noak Hill - St. George's Hospital	10	10	20	Arriva Sth Cou.	GY	SB120/Cadet
257	Walthamstow - Stratford	14	8	12	Stagecoach	WH	Tri/ALX400
258	Watford - South Harrow	11	15	30	Arriva Shires	GR	DB250/Gem
259	Edmonton Green - King's Cross	20	8	10	First	NP	B7TL/Pres
							B9TL/Gem2
							Tri/Pres
260	Golders Green - White City	16	12	15	Metroline	AC	B7TL/Pres
261	Princess Royal University Hospital - Lewisham	11	12	15	Metrobus	MB	N94/Omni
262	East Beckton - Stratford	12	10	15	Stagecoach	WH	Tri/ALX400
263	Barnet Hospital - Holloway	15	10	12	Metroline	PB	Env400
264	Croydon - St. George's Hospital	14	10	15	Arriva	CN	DB250/Gem
265	Tolworth - Putney Bridge	11	12	15	London United	TV	Dar/Point
266	Brent Cross - Hammersmith	25	8	10	Metroline	W	Tri/ALX400
267	Fulwell - Hammersmith	16	11	15	London United	FW	N94/Omni
							N230/Omni
							Tri/ALX400
268	Golders Green - Finchley Road	6	12	12	Arriva Shires	GR	SB120/Cadet
269	Bexleyheath - Bromley	14	10	15	Stagecoach	TB	Tri/ALX400
270	Mitcham - Putney Bridge	13	10	12	Go-Ahead	AL	B7TL/Gem
							B7TL/Pres
271	Highgate - Moorgate	12	8	12	Metroline	HT	B7TL/Pres
							Tri/Pres
272	Chiswick (Grove Park) - Shepherd's Bush	8	15	15	London United	PK	Env200
273	Petts Wood - Lewisham	8	20	30	Stagecoach	TL	Dar/ALX200
							Env200
274	Lancaster Gate - Islington	17	8	8	Metroline	KC	Env200
275	Barkingside - Walthamstow St. James Street Stn.	10	12	20	Arriva	DX	B7TL/Gem
276	Stoke Newington - Newham General Hospital	18	12	15	Go-Ahead	SI	Env200

A 10.2m ALX200, 34313, heads through Homerton. Stagecoach lost this route to Go-Ahead on 17th September 2011 and it converted to Enviro200s.

No.	Route	PVR	Freq		Operator	Garage	Type Used
277	Highbury - Leamouth	22	11	7	Stagecoach	BW	Tri/ALX400
279	Waltham Cross - Manor House	31	6	10	Arriva	E	B7TL/Gem
							DB250/ALX400
							DB250/Pres

No.	Route	PVR	Freq		Operator	Garage	Type Used
280	Belmont - Tooting St. George's Hospital	14	10	12	Go-Ahead	AL	B7TL/Gem B7TL/Pres
281	Tolworth - Hounslow	23	8	12	London United	FW	N94/Omni N230/Omni Tri/ALX400
282	Mount Vernon Hospital - Ealing Hospital	16	12	15	First	G	Env400 Tri/Pres
283	East Acton - Barn Elms	16	8	12	London United	PK	Versa
284	Grove Park Cemetery - Lewisham	10	12	20	Metrobus	MB	N94/Est
285	Heathrow Airport Central - Kingston	19	10	12	London United	HH	Env200
286	Sidcup - Greenwich	13	12	15	Arriva Sth Cou.	DT	Env200
287	Abbey Wood Lane - Barking	7	15	20	Stagecoach	RM	Env400
288	Broadfields - Queensbury	6	10	15	Arriva Shires	GR	SB120/Cadet
289	Purley - Elmers End	8	15	20	Arriva	TH	Dar/Point DB250/ALX400 SB120/Cadet
290	Staines - Twickenham	6	20	20	London United	FW	Dar/Point
291	Woodlands Estate - Queen Elizabeth Hospital	7	10	15	Stagecoach	PD	Dar/Point Env200
292	Borehamwood - Colindale	9	15	20	Lon. Sovereign	BT	B7TL/Pres B7TL/Vyk N94/Omni N230/Omni
293	Epsom General Hospital - Morden	6	20	30	Metrobus	C	N230/Omni
294	Noak Hill - Havering Park	11	12	20	Stagecoach	NS	Tri/ALX400

A different side of Shepherds Bush Green, beside the Empire theatre. TNA33350, sporting full First Group branding, passes a London United Enviro200.

No.	Route	PVR	Freq		Operator	Garage	Type Used
295	Ladbroke Grove - Clapham Junction	19	8	12	First	X	Tri/ALX400 Tri/Pres
296	Romford - Ilford	6	20	30	Stagecoach	NS	Env200
297	Willesden Garage - Ealing Haven Green	16	10	12	Metroline	PA	Env400 N230/Olym
298	Potters Bar - Arnos Grove	5	20	30	Arriva	WN	SB120/Cadet

No.	Route	PVR	Freq		Operator	Garage	Type Used
299	Cockfosters - Muswell Hill	7	15	30	First	NP	Env200
300	East Ham - Canning Town	12	12	20	Go-Ahead	SI	Env200
302	Mill Hill - Kensal Rise	16	8	12	Metroline	AC	B7TL/Pres
303	Colindale - Edgware	6	15	20	Arriva Shires	GR	SB120/Cadet
305	Kingsbury - Edgware	4	15	20	Arriva Shires	GR	SB120/Cadet
307	Brimsdown - Arkley Hotel	14	10	20	Arriva	E	DB250/Pres
308	Wanstead - Clapton Park Millfields	9	15	30	First	LI	Dar/Cap
							Dar/Nimb
309	Canning Town Station - London Chest Hospital	8	12	15	First	LI	Dar/Cap
312	South Croydon - Norwood Junction	6	12	20	Arriva	TC	Dar/Point
							Env200
313	Potters Bar - Chingford	7	20	30	Arriva	E	SB120/Cadet
314	New Addington - Eltham	12	15	30	Stagecoach	TB	Dar/Point
315	West Norwood Station - Balham	4	20	30	Go-Ahead	SW	Dar/Point
316	Cricklewood - White City	18	8	12	Metroline	W	Env200
317	Waltham Cross - Enfield	5	20	30	Arriva	E	DB250/ALX400
318	North Middlesex Hospital - Stamford Hill	5	20	30	Arriva	AR	Dar/Point
319	Streatham Hill - Sloane Square	19	8	12	Arriva	BN	DB250/ALX400
320	Biggin Hill Valley - Catford	12	12	20	Metrobus	MB	N94/Omni
							N230/Omni
321	Foots Cray - New Cross	10	8	12	Go-Ahead	NX	B7TL/Pres
322	Crystal Palace - Clapham Common	8	15	20	Abellio	BC	Dar/Point
323	Canning Town Station - Mile End	4	15	20	Stagecoach	WH	Dar/ALX200
							Env200
324	Stanmore - Brent Cross	6	20	20	Lon. Sovereign	BT	Env200
325	Prince Regent Station - Beckton	11	12	20	Arriva	DX	Env200
326	Barnet - Brent Cross	14	12	15	Metroline	PA	Env200
327	Waltham Cross - Waltham Cross	1	30	-	Arriva	E	Dar/Point
328	Golders Green - Chelsea	27	7	10	First	X	B7TL/Gem
							Gem2 HEV
329	Enfield - Turnpike Lane Station	17	7	8	Arriva	AD	DB250/Pres
							Env400
330	Forest Gate - Canning Town	8	12	20	Stagecoach	WH	Tri/ALX400
331	Ruislip - Uxbridge	7	20	30	First	UX	Env200
332	Neasden - Paddington	15	10	12	Metroline	W	Env400
333	Tooting - Elephant & Castle	14	10	12	Go-Ahead	SW	B7TL/Gem
							B7TL/Pres
							Env400
336	Locksbottom - Catford	7	20	30	Metrobus	MB	Dar/Est
337	Richmond - Clapham Junction	13	12	15	Go-Ahead	SW	Env400
339	Bow Fish Island - Shadwell Station	4	15	20	First	LI	Env200
340	Edgware - Harrow	9	12	20	Arriva Shires	GR	DB250/ALX400
341	Lea Valley - Waterloo County Hall	21	10	12	Arriva	LV	Env400
343	New Cross Gate - City Hall	22	7	10	Abellio	WL	B7TL/Gem
344	Clapham Junction - Bishopsgate	23	7	10	Abellio	QB	Env400
							Tri/ALX400
345	Peckham - South Kensington	24	8	10	Go-Ahead	SW	B7TL/Pres
							Env400
346	Upminster Park Estate - Upminster	2	15	-	Arriva Sth Cou.	GY	SB120/Cadet
347	Ockendon Station - Romford (10am - 4pm only)	1	120	-	Go-Ahead	BE	Env200
349	Ponders End - Stamford Hill	14	8	12	Arriva	E	B7TL/Gem
							DB250/ALX400
							DB250/Pres
350	Hayes - Heathrow Airport Terminal 5	8	12	20	Abellio	WS	Env200
352	Lower Sydenham - Bromley	5	20	-	Metrobus	MB	Dar/Point
353	Ramsden - Addington Interchange	6	15	30	Metrobus	MB	N94/Omni
354	Penge - Bromley	5	25	-	Stagecoach	TB	Env200
355	Mitcham - Brixton	11	12	15	Go-Ahead	AL	Dar/Point
							E200/Est

No.	Route	PVR	Freq		Operator	Garage	Type Used
356	Shirley - Sydenham Hill	6	20	30	Stagecoach	TL	Env200
357	Chingford Hatch - Whipps Cross	7	15	30	First	NP	Tri/Pres
358	Orpington Station - Crystal Palace	16	12	20	Metrobus	MB	CN94/Omni
359	Addington Interchange - Selsdon (10am - 3pm only)	1	35	-	Metrobus	C	Dar/Point Man240/Env200
360	Albert Hall - Elephant & Castle	11	12	15	Go-Ahead	Q	Dar/Point SB120/Ecity
362	Grange Hill - Little Heath King George Hospital	3	30	30	Go-Ahead	BE	Env200
363	Crystal Palace - Elephant & Castle	12	10	15	Go-Ahead	PM	B7TL/Pres B9TL/Gem2 Env400
364	Dagenham East - Ilford	13	10	15	Go-Ahead	BE	Env200
365	Mardyke Estate - Havering Park	10	12	20	First	DM	Env400
366	Redbridge - Beckton	15	12	20	Stagecoach	BK	Env200
367	Bromley - Croydon	9	20	30	Metrobus	MB	Dar/Est
368	Chadwell Heath - Harts Lane Estate	7	12	20	First	DM	Env200
370	Lakeside - Romford	10	15	30	Arriva Sth Cou.	GY	Env200

The 10.2m Enviro200 is the most numerous single-decker in London. Fulwell garage's DE26 passes the posh shops of George Street, Richmond.

No.	Route	PVR	Freq		Operator	Garage	Type Used
371	Kingston - Richmond	14	9	12	London United	FW	Dar/Point Env200 Env200H N230/Omni
372	Lakeside - Hornchurch	6	20	30	Stagecoach	RM	Env200
375	Passingford Bridge - Romford	1	90	-	Arriva Sth Cou.	GY	Env200
376	Beckton - East Ham	8	15	30	Go-Ahead	BE	Env200
377	Oakwood - Ponders End	3	30	-	Arriva	E	Dar/Point
379	Yardley Lane Estate - Chingford	2	15	30	Arriva	EC	Dar/Point
380	Belmarsh - Lewisham	11	12	15	Stagecoach	TL	Dar/ALX200 Dar/Point

No.	Route	PVR	Freq		Operator	Garage	Type Used
381	Peckham - Waterloo County Hall	17	11	12	Abellio	WL	B7TL/Gem
382	Mill Hill East - Southgate	10	15	30	Arriva	EC	Dar/Point
383	Barnet - Woodside Park Station	3	30	-	Metroline	PB	Env200
384	Quinta Drive - Cockfosters	8	15	30	Metroline	PB	Env200
385	Chingford - Crooked Billet	1	60	-	CT Plus	HK	Dar/Point
386	Woolwich - Blackheath Village	10	15	20	Stagecoach	PD	Dar/Point Env200
387	Little Heath - Barking Reach	10	12	20	Stagecoach	BK	Tri/ALX400

HTL 8, one of thirteen Trident/Myllenium Lolynes operated by CT Plus, passes Mansion House. In the distance, the top of the famous 'Gherkin' rises above the demolition of Bucklersbury House.

No.	Route	PVR	Freq		Operator	Garage	Type Used
388	Hackney Wick - Embankment Station	13	10	12	CT Plus	HK	Tri/Loly Tri/Olym Tri/Pres
389	Barnet - Barnet Salisbury Road (11am - 4pm only)	1	60	-	First	NP	Env200
390	Archway - Notting Hill Gate	20	8	12	Metroline	HT	B7TL/Pres
391	Richmond - Sands End	17	10	12	London United	V	Versa
393	Clapton - Chalk Farm	10	12	20	Arriva	AE CT	Env200 Env200
394	Homerton Hospital - Islington	10	12	20	CT Plus	HK	Dar/Nimb Env200
395	Westway Cross - Harrow	4	22	30	Metroline	PA	Env200
396	Little Heath King George Hospital - Ilford	5	20	20	Stagecoach	BK	Versa
397	Debden - Crooked Billet	5	30	30	Arriva	EC	Dar/ALX200 Dar/Point
398	Ruislip - Wood End	3	30	-	Lon.Sovereign	SO	Dar/Point Env200
399	Barnet - Barnet (10am - 3pm only)	1	60	-	First	NP	Env200
401	Thamesmead - Bexleyheath	7	15	30	Go-Ahead	BX	B7TL/Pres B9TL/Gem
403	Warlingham - Croydon	7	12	20	Arriva	CN	DB250/Gem
404	Caterham-on-the-Hill - Coulsdon	1	60	-	Quality Line	EB	Solo
405	Redhill - Croydon	9	15	30	Metrobus	C	N230/Omni

Enviro200 8520 heads along Croydon Road in Wallington. The bus is based only a mile away at Abellio's Beddington garage – one of the unlovely constructions on industrial estates.

No.	Route	PVR	Freq		Operator	Garage	Type Used
406	Epsom - Kingston	4	30	30	Quality Line	EB	Env400
407	Caterham - Sutton	12	15	20	Abellio	BC	Env200
410	Wallington - Crystal Palace	19	8	15	Arriva	CN	Dar/ALX200 SB120/Cadet
411	West Molesey - Kingston	6	20	30	Quality Line	EB	Versa
412	Purley - Croydon	8	15	20	Arriva	TC	DB250/ALX400 DB250/Gem
413	Sutton - Morden	7	15	30	Go-Ahead	A	Dar/Point E200/Est
414	Putney Bridge Station - Maida Hill	17	8	12	Abellio	QB	Env400
415	Tulse Hill - Elephant & Castle	7	12	20	Arriva	N	B7TL/ALX400 DB250/ALX400
417	Crystal Palace - Clapham Common	11	9	15	Arriva	N	B7TL/ALX400
418	Epsom - Kingston	4	30	30	Quality Line	EB	Env400
419	Richmond - Hammersmith	7	15	30	London United	NC	Dar/Point
422	Bexleyheath Bus Garage - North Greenwich	16	10	20	Go-Ahead	BX	B9TL/Gem2
423	Heathrow Airport (Terminal 5) - Hounslow	7	20	30	London United	HH	Env200
424	Putney Heath - Fulham Craven Cottage	5	30	-	Go-Ahead	AF	Dar/Point
425	Clapton Nightingale Road - Stratford	9	12	15	Go-Ahead	SI	B7TL/Pres B9TL/MCV N94/Omni N230/Omni
427	Uxbridge - Acton	22	8	10	First	HS	B9TL/Gem2
428	Bluewater - Erith	7	15	30	Arriva Sth Cou.	DT	Env200 SB180/Evo
430	Roehampton - South Kensington	15	8	10	Go-Ahead	AF	B7TL/Gem
432	Anerley Station - Brixton	9	12	15	Arriva	N	B7TL/ALX400 DB250/ALX400
434	Rickman Hill - Whyteleafe Station	3	30	-	Abellio	BC	Env200

No.	Route	PVR	Freq		Operator	Garage	Type Used
436	Lewisham - Paddington	26	8	12	Go-Ahead	NX	Citartic
440	Stonebridge Park Station - Gunnersbury	10	15	20	London United	PK	Env200
444	Chingford - Turnpike Lane Station	8	15	20	Arriva	EC	Dar/ALX200
							Dar/Point
							SB120/Cadet
450	Lower Sydenham - West Croydon	11	12	20	Arriva	CN	Dar/Point
452	Kensal Rise - Wandsworth Road Station	20	8	12	Abellio	QB	Env400

Route 453 will lose its bendys in the middle of November 2011. The previous March, MAL99 enjoys an unseasonal heatwave on the stand at Marylebone.

No.	Route	PVR	Freq		Operator	Garage	Type Used
453	Deptford - Marylebone Station	23	8	10	Go-Ahead	MW	Citartic
455	Old Lodge Lane - Wallington	9	20	30	Arriva	CN	SB120/Cadet
460	North Finchley - Willesden	12	13	15	Metroline	AC	B7TL/Pres
462	Hainault - Ilford	8	15	30	Arriva	DX	Dar/Point
463	Coulsdon South Station - Pollards Hill	8	20	30	Quality Line	EB	Solo
464	Tatsfield - New Addington	3	30	60	Metrobus	MB	Dar/Point
465	Dorking - Kingston	5	30	60	Metrobus	CY	Env200
466	Caterham-on-the-Hill - Addington Interchange	18	10	15	Arriva	TC	Env400
467	Hook - Epsom	2	60	-	Quality Line	EB	Env400
468	South Croydon - Elephant & Castle	26	8	12	Go-Ahead	Q	B7TL/Gem
							B7TL/Pres
469	Erith - Queen Elizabeth Hospital	8	15	20	Stagecoach	PD	Versa
470	Epsom - Colliers Wood	7	30	-	Quality Line	EB	Solo
472	Thamesmead - North Greenwich	20	6	10	Stagecoach	PD	Tri/ALX400
473	North Woolwich - Stratford	10	10	15	Stagecoach	WH	Tri/ALX400
474	Manor Park - Canning Town	12	12	15	Go-Ahead	SI	B9TL/Gem2
							B9TL/MCV
							N94/Omni
476	Northumberland Park - Euston	21	8	12	First	NP	B7TL/Pres
							B9TL/Gem2
							Tri/Pres

No.	Route	PVR	Freq		Operator	Garage	Type Used
481	Isleworth West Middlesex Hospital - Kingston	2	60	-	Abellio	TF	Dar/Point Env200
482	Southall - Heathrow Airport Terminal 5	8	20	30	London United	HH	Env400H N230/Omni
484	Lewisham - Camberwell	12	10	15	Abellio	WL	Env200
485	Wandsworth - Hammersmith	3	30	-	Go-Ahead	PL	Dar/Point
486	Bexleyheath - North Greenwich	15	8	12	Go-Ahead	BX	Env400
487	South Harrow - Willesden Junction Station	9	15	20	First	WJ	Env200
488	Clapton - Bromley-by-Bow	9	12	15	Stagecoach	WH	Env200
490	Heathrow Airport Terminal 5 - Richmond	13	12	20	Abellio	TF	Dar/Nimb Dar/Point
491	Waltham Cross - North Middlesex Hospital	10	15	30	Arriva	E	Env200
492	Bluewater - Sidcup	6	30	30	Arriva Sth Cou.	DT	DB250/Gem
493	Richmond - Tooting St. George's Hospital	17	12	20	London United	NC	Env200

One of 124 standard diesel Enviro400s delivered to Stagecoach in 2011, 19735 is part of the Romford allocation for route 496. In the bare state in which it was delivered, the bus approaches the stand at Harold Wood station. Despite the new influx, ALX400s still appear on this route.

No.	Route	PVR	Freq		Operator	Garage	Type Used
496	Harold Wood - Romford	8	15	20	Stagecoach	NS	Env400 Tri/ALX400
498	Brentwood - Romford	3	30	60	First	DM	Env200
499	Gallows Corner - Heath Park Estate	4	30	30	Arriva Sth Cou.	GY	Env200 SB120/Cadet
507	Victoria - Waterloo	15	6	12	Go-Ahead	RA	Citaro
521	Waterloo - London Bridge (Mon-Fri only)	31	5	-	Go-Ahead	RA MW	Citaro Citaro
541	Keir Hardie Estate - Canning Town	4	10	12	Stagecoach	WH	Tri/ALX400
549	Loughton Station - South Woodford	1	60	-	Go-Ahead	SI	Env200
603	Muswell Hill - Swiss Cottage (Mon-Fri only 2 Trips)	2			Metroline	HT	Tri/Pres
607	Uxbridge - White City	20	10	12	First	UX	Tri/Pres
A10	Uxbridge - Heathrow Airport Central	5	15	30	First	UX	Env200
B11	Thamesmead - Bexleyheath Bus Garage	7	15	30	Go-Ahead	BX	Env200
B12	Joydens Wood - Erith	6	20	-	Arriva Sth Cou.	DT	Env200 SB180/Evo

No.	Route	PVR	Freq		Operator	Garage	Type Used
B13	New Eltham - Bexleyheath	5	15	30	Arriva Sth Cou.	DT	SB120/Cadet
B14	Orpington - Bexleyheath	5	30	30	Metrobus	MB	Env200
B15	Bexleyheath - Horn Park	5	20	30	Arriva Sth Cou.	DT	SB120/Cadet SB180/Evo
B16	Kidbrooke Station - Bexleyheath Bus Garage	8	15	30	Go-Ahead	BX	Env200
C1	White City - Victoria	14	10	12	London United	PK	Env200
C2	Parliament Hill - Victoria	17	8	8	Metroline	HT	B7TL/Pres Tri/Pres
C3	Clapham Junction - Earl's Court	12	8	12	Abellio	QB	Tri/ALX400
C10	Canada Water - Victoria	14	12	20	Abellio	QB	Env200
C11	Brent Cross - Archway	20	8	12	Metroline	PA	Dar/Point Env200
D3	Crossharbour - Bethnal Green	15	10	15	Stagecoach	WH	Env200
D6	Crossharbour - Hackney	16	8	15	Go-Ahead	SI	Env200
D7	Poplar - Mile End	11	8	15	Go-Ahead	SI	B9TL/Gem2
D8	Crossharbour - Stratford	8	12	20	Go-Ahead	SI	Env200
E1	Greenford - Ealing Haven Green	7	10	10	First	G	Env400
E2	Greenford - Brentford	15	9	12	Metroline	AH	B9TL/Gem2
E3	Greenford - Chiswick	26	7	10	First	G	Env400
E5	Toplocks - Perivale	11	12	20	First	G	Env200
E6	Greenford Station - Bulls Bridge	12	10	15	Metroline	PA	Env200
E7	Ruislip - Ealing	10	12	20	First	G	Env200

A mixture of Brentford-based single-deckers work route E8. On this occasion, E200 Dart Evolution DM970 appears at Haven Green, Ealing.

No.	Route	PVR	Freq		Operator	Garage	Type Used
E8	Brentford - Ealing	10	9	10	Metroline	AH	Env200 E200/Evo Temp Hybrid
E9	Yeading Barnhill Estate - Ealing	8	12	20	First	G	Env200
E10	Islip Manor - Ealing	7	15	20	First	G	Env200
E11	Greenford - Ealing Common	5	20	30	London United	PK	Env200
EL1	Thames View Estate - Ilford Hill	7	12	20	Go-Ahead	BE	B9TL/Gem2
EL2	Dagenham Dock - Ilford Hill	7	12	20	Go-Ahead	BE	B9TL/Gem2

No.	Route	PVR	Freq		Operator		Garage	Type Used
G1	Streatham High Road - Shaftesbury Estate	9	20	30	Go-Ahead	PL		Dar/Point
H2	Golders Green - Golders Green (circular Trip)	3	12	15	Arriva Shires	GR		Solo
H3	Golders Green - Golders Green (circular Trip)	1	60	-	Arriva Shires	GR		Solo
H9	Harrow - Harrow (circular Trip)	8	10	20	Lon. Sovereign	SO		Dar/Point Env200
H10	Harrow - Harrow (circular Trip)	7	10	20	Lon. Sovereign	SO		Dar/Point Env200
H11	Mount Vernon Hospital - Harrow	6	15	20	Lon. Sovereign	SO		Env200
H12	Stanmore - South Harrow	12	10	15	Metroline	HD		B7TL/Pres
H13	St. Vincent's Park - Ruislip Lido	5	20	30	Lon. Sovereign	SO		Dar/Point Env200

London Sovereign's Dart Pointer 2, DPS2, pulls away from a stop in Harrow High Street. The Pointers were replaced by Enviro200s on 3rd September 2011.

H14	Hatch End - Northwick Park Hospital	7	10	15	Lon. Sovereign	SO		Env200
H17	Wembley - Harrow	6	15	20	Lon. Sovereign	SO		Env200
H18	Harrow - Harrow (circular Trip - buses shared with H19)	5	30	30	Arriva Shires	GR		Dar/Point SB120/Cadet
H19	Harrow - Harrow (circular Trip - buses shared with H18)	5	30	30	Arriva Shires	GR		Dar/Point SB120/Cadet
H20	Ivybridge - Hounslow Civic Centre	5	12	20	Abellio	TF		Dar/Point
H22	Hounslow - Richmond	11	12	20	London United	HH		Dar/Point
H25	Butts Farm - Hatton Cross	7	15	20	Abellio	TF		Dar/Nimb
H26	Sparrow Farm - Hatton Cross	4	20	30	Abellio	TF		Env200
H28	Bulls Bridge - Osterley	8	20	30	Abellio	WS		Dar/Point
H32	Southall - Hounslow	12	10	15	London United	AV		B7TL/ALX400 B7TL/Pres N230/Omni
H37	Hounslow - Richmond	15	6	8	London United	AV		Dar/Point Tempo

No.	Route	PVR	Freq		Operator	Garage	Type Used
H91	Hounslow West - Hammersmith	14	10	15	London United	HH	N230/Omni
H98	Hayes End - Hounslow	15	8	15	London United	AV	Env200
K1	New Malden - Kingston	9	15	20	London United	TV	Env200
K2	Hook Library - Kingston Hospital	10	11	15	London United	TV	Dar/Point
K3	Esher - Roehampton Vale	10	15	30	London United	TV	Dar/Point
K4	Mansfield Estate - Kingston Hospital	4	30	-	London United	TV	Dar/Point
K5	Ham - Morden	3	60	-	Quality Line	EB	Solo
P4	Lewisham - Brixton	10	12	12	Stagecoach	TL	Dar/Point
P5	Nine Elms - Elephant & Castle	8	15	20	Go-Ahead	Q	Env200
P12	Brockley Rise - Surrey Quays	12	10	20	Go-Ahead	PM	Dar/Point
P13	Streatham - New Cross Gate	8	20	30	Abellio	BC	Dar/Point
PR2	The Paddocks - Willesden Junction Station	5	30	-	First	WJ	Dar/Cap
R1	Green Street Green - Grovelands	7	15	30	Metrobus	MB	Dar/Cap Dar/Point
R2	Melody Road - Petts Wood Station	4	30	-	Metrobus	MB	Man240/Est
R3	Chelsfield Village - Princess Royal University Hospital	4	30	60	Metrobus	MB	Dar/Cap
R4	Pauls Cray Hill - Princess Royal University Hospital	5	20	60	Metrobus	MB	Dar/Cap
R5	Orpington - Orpington (circ. Trip - buses shared with R10)	1	120	-	Metrobus	MB	Dar/Point
R6	Orpington - St Mary Cray	2	30	60	Metrobus	MB	Dar/Cap
R7	Orpington - Bickley	1	60	-	Metrobus	MB	Dar/Point
R8	Orpington - Biggin Hill	1	70	-	Metrobus	MB	Solo
R9	Orpington - Orpington (circular Trip)	3	12	20	Metrobus	MB	Env200
R10	Orpington - Orpington (circ. Trip - buses shared with R5)	1	120	-	Metrobus	MB	Dar/Point
R11	Green Street Green - Sidcup Queen Mary's Hospital	7	15	30	Metrobus	MB	Dar/Cap Dar/Point
R68	Hampton Court - Kew	10	15	15	Abellio	TF	Env200
R70	Manor Circus - Nurserylands	11	10	20	Abellio	TF	Env200
RV1	Tower Gateway Station - Covent Garden	8	10	20	First	LI	Env200 HYDRO

Exactly one week after entering service, hydrogen fuel cell bus WSH62991 is still behaving itself on the RV1. However, the Enviro200s borrowed from Uxbridge garage to cover for the late arrival of 'zero emissions' buses continue to hang around on the route, along with a variety of other types from Lea Interchange garage.

Route S3 provides a handy link between Sutton Hospital and the Royal Marsden, although whether it's used to transfer patients is open to doubt. SD40 pauses on its way to the Sutton end of the route. Photo: Adam Murray

No.	Route	PVR	Freq		Operator	Garage	Type Used
S1	Banstead - Mitcham	8	20	30	Quality Line	EB	E200/Est
S3	Sutton Hospital - Malden Manor Station	6	20	-	Quality Line	EB	Dar/ALX200 Dar/Myl Env200
S4	Roundshaw - St. Helier Station	3	30	-	Quality Line	EB	E200/Est Solo
T31	New Addington - Forestdale	8	8	15	Arriva	TC	Env200
T32	New Addington - Addington Interchange	3	15	30	Metrobus	C	Man240/Env200
T33	Addington Interchange - Croydon	10	8	15	Metrobus	C	Dar/Point
U1	West Drayton - Ruislip	8	15	30	First	UX	Dar/Nimb Env200
U2	Brunel University - Uxbridge	8	10	20	First	UX	Dar/Nimb Env200
U3	Heathrow Airport Central - Uxbridge	10	12	20	First	UX	Dar/Nimb Env200
U4	Hayes - Uxbridge	14	8	20	First	UX	Tri/Pres
U5	Hayes - Uxbridge	11	12	20	First	UX	Dar/Nimb Env200
U7	Hayes - Uxbridge	4	30	30	Abellio	WS	Dar/Point
U9	Harefield Hospital - Uxbridge	3	20	60	Arriva Shires	WB	Dar/Point
U10	Heathfield Rise - Uxbridge	2	60	-	First	UX	Dar/Nimb Env200

No.	Route	PVR	Freq		Operator	Garage	Type Used
W3	Northumberland Park - Finsbury Park	20	6	10	Arriva	WN	B7TL/Gem DB250/ALX400 DB250/Pres
W4	Oakthorpe Park - Ferry Lane Estate	11	10	15	First	NP	Env200
W5	Archway - Harringay	7	12	20	CT Plus	HK	Solo
W6	Southgate - Edmonton Green	8	10	15	First	LV	Dar/Point
W7	Muswell Hill - Finsbury Park	16	6	8	Metroline	HT	B7TL/Pres Tri/Pres
W8	Chase Farm Hospital - Picketts Lock	14	8	12	Metroline	PB	Tri/Pres
W9	Chase Farm Hospital - Southgate	8	15	30	Metroline	PB	Dar/Point Env200
W10	Crews Hill - Enfield (11am-3pm)	1	60	-	First	NP	Env200

The limited stop X26 is currently operated by Metrobus with these single-deck Scanias, but Quality Line will take over the contract from April 2012.

No.	Route	PVR	Freq		Operator	Garage	Type Used
W11	Chingford Hall Estate - Walthamstow	7	10	15	First	LI	Dar/Cap
W12	Wanstead - Coppermill Lane	6	20	30	CT Plus	HK	Solo
W13	Woodford Wells - Leytonstone	5	15	30	CT Plus	HK	E200/Est
W14	Woodford Bridge - Leyton	10	15	20	Arriva	EC	Dar/ALX200 Dar/Point
W15	Cogan Avenue - Hackney	21	8	12	Arriva	EC	Dar/ALX200 Dar/Point SB120/Cadet
W16	Chingford Mount - Leytonstone Station	9	12	20	Arriva	EC	Dar/Point
W19	Ilford - Walthamstow	8	20	30	Go-Ahead	BE	Dar/Evo
X26	West Croydon - Heathrow Airport Central	9	30	30	Metrobus	C	CN94/Omni
X68	West Croydon - Russell Square (Mon-Fri peak hours)	7	20	-	Go-Ahead	Q	B7TL/Gem B7TL/Pres

Night Buses

No.	Route	PVR	Freq mf	sat	Operator	Garage	Type Used
N1	Thamesmead - Tottenham Court Road	9	30	20	Go-Ahead	BV	B7TL/Gem
						MW	B7TL/Gem
N2	Crystal Palace - Trafalgar Square	5	30	20	Arriva	MW	B7TL/ALX400
N3	Bromley - Oxford Circus	10	30	15	Abellio	BC	Tri/ALX400
						QB	Env400
N5	Edgware - Trafalgar Square	17	15	10	Metroline	EW	B7TL/Pres
							Env400
						HT	B7TL/Pres
N7	Northolt - Russell Square	7	30	30	Metroline	PV	N230/Olym
N8	Hainault - Oxford Circus	17	20	10	Stagecoach	BW	Tri/ALX400
N9	Heathrow Airport Terminal 5 - Aldwych	17	20	10	London United	AV	B7TL/ALX400
							B7TL/Pres
							N230/Omni
N11	Ealing - Liverpool Street	7	30	30	Go-Ahead	SW	B7TL/Gem
N13	North Finchley - Aldwych	14	15	15	Lon.Sovereign	BT	N94/Omni
							N230/Omni
N15	Romford - PicCadilly Circus	8	15	12	Stagecoach	BK	Env400
							Tri/ALX400
N16	Edgware - Victoria	7	20	20	Metroline	EW	B7TL/Pres
							Env400
						HD	B7TL/Pres
N18	Harrow Weald - Trafalgar Square	15	15	10	First	WJ	B9TL/Gem2
N19	Clapham Junction - Finsbury Park	7	30	30	Arriva	BN	DB250/Gem
N20	Barnet - Trafalgar Square	14	30	12	Metroline	HT	Tri/Pres
						PB	Tri/Pres
N21	Bexleyheath - Trafalgar Square	5	30	30	Go-Ahead	NX	B7TL/Pres
							B9TL/Gem2
						BX	B9TL/Gem2
N22	Fulwell - PicCadilly Circus	8	30	20	Go-Ahead	AF	B7TL/Gem
N26	Chingford - Trafalgar Square	8	20	20	First	LI	Tri/ALX400
N28	Wandsworth - Camden Town	4	60	30	First	X	B7TL/Gem
N29	Enfield - Trafalgar Square	24	12	6	Arriva	EC	Citartic
N31	Clapham Junction - Camden Town	4	60	30	First	X	B7TL/Gem
N35	Clapham Junction - Tottenham Court Road Station	11	30	15	Abellio	QB	Env400
N38	Walthamstow - Victoria	26	12	12	Arriva	CT	DB250/ALX400
N41	Tottenham Hale - Trafalgar Square	5	30	30	Arriva	AR	B7TL/ALX400
							DB250/ALX400
N44	Sutton - Aldwych	9	30	20	Go-Ahead	SW	B7TL/Gem
							B7TL/Pres
N47	St. Mary Cray Station - Trafalgar Square	10	30	20	Stagecoach	TL	Tri/ALX400
N52	Willesden - Victoria	4	30	30	Metroline	AC	B7TL/Pres
N55	Woodford Wells - Oxford Circus	11	30	15	Stagecoach	T	Tri/ALX400
N63	Crystal Palace - King's Cross	8	30	15	Go-Ahead	PM	B9TL/Gem2
N64	Homestead Way - Thornton Heath Bus Garage	3	30	30	Metrobus	C	N230/Omni
N68	Old Coulsdon - Tottenham Court Road Station	6	30	30	Go-Ahead	Q	B7TL/Gem
N73	Walthamstow - Victoria	10	30	15	Arriva	SF	Gem2Int
							B5L/Gem2
N74	Danebury Avenue - Baker Street	5	30	30	Go-Ahead	AF	B7TL/Gem
N76	Northumberland Park - Waterloo	5	30	30	Arriva	AR	B5L/Gem
							B7TL/ALX400
N86	Dagnam Park Drive - Stratford	5	30	30	Stagecoach	NS	Tri/ALX400
N87	Kingston - Aldwych	16	15	10	Go-Ahead	SW	B7TL/Gem
							B7TL/Pres
N89	Erith - Trafalgar Square	9	30	20	Go-Ahead	BX	B9TL/Gem2
							Env400

No.	Route	PVR	Freq mf	sat	Operator	Garage	Type Used
N91	Cockfosters - Trafalgar Square	14	30	15	Metroline	HT	Env400
						PB	Env400
N97	Hammersmith - Trafalgar Square	9	20	10	London United	S	B7TL/ALX400
							N230/Pres
N98	Stanmore - Holborn	8	15	10	Metroline	EW	B7TL/Pres
							Env400
						AC	B7TL/Pres
N109	Croydon - Oxford Circus	9	20	20	Arriva	TH	DB250/ALX400
							Env400
N133	Mitcham - Liverpool Street Station	6	20	20	Arriva	TC	Env400
N136	Chislehurst War Memorial - Oxford Circus	10	30	20	Stagecoach	TL	Tri/ALX400
N137	Crystal Palace - Oxford Circus	10	30	15	Arriva	N	B7TL/ALX400
N155	Morden -Aldwych	18	15	8	Go-Ahead	AL	B7TL/Gem
							B7TL/Pres
						A	Tri/Olym
N171	Hither Green - Tottenham Court Road	5	30	30	Go-Ahead	NX	B9TL/Gem2
N207	Uxbridge - Holborn	21	15	10	First	HS	B9TL/Gem2
						UX	Tri/Pres
N253	Aldgate - Tottenham Court Road Station	13	15	12	Arriva	SF	B7TL/Gem
N279	Waltham Cross - Trafalgar Square	15	20	12	Arriva	E	B7TL/Gem
							DB250/Pres
N343	New Cross Gate - Trafalgar Square	5	30	30	Abellio	WL	B7TL/Gem
N381	Peckham - Trafalgar Square	4	30	30	Abellio	WL	B7TL/Gem
N550	Canning Town - Trafalgar Square	5	30	30	Stagecoach	U	Tri/ALX400
N551	Gallions Reach - Trafalgar Square	6	30	30	Go-Ahead	SI	N94/Omni

School Buses

No.	Route	Operator	Garage	Type Used
601	Thamesmead - Dartford Heath	Stagecoach	PD	Tri/ALX400
602	Thamesmead - Bexleyheath Grammar School	Stagecoach	PD	Tri/ALX400
605	Edgware - Mill Hill County School	Metroline	EW	B7TL/Pres
				Env400
606	Queensbury - Ravenscroft School	Metroline	EW	B7TL/Pres
				Env400
608	Gallows Corner - Shenfield High School	First	DM	B7TL/Pres
609	Hammersmith - Harrodian School	Metroline	AH	Env200
611	Stonebridge Park - East Finchley Cemetery	Metroline	PV	N230/Olym
				Tri/Pres
612	Sanderstead - Wallington County Grammar School	Metrobus	C	N230/Omni
				N94/Omni
613	Worcester Park - Glenthorne High School	London United	TV	Tri/ALX400
616	Green Dragon Lane - Edmonton Green	First	NP	Tri/Pres
617	Turnpike Lane Station - St. Ignatius College	Arriva	WN	DB250/ALX400
621	Lewisham - Crown Woods School	Go-Ahead	NX	B7TL/Pres
624	Grove Park - Crown Woods School	Stagecoach	TL	Tri/ALX400
625	Plumstead Common - Chislehurst	Stagecoach	PD	Tri/ALX400
626	Finchley - Potters Bar Dame Alice Owen's School	Metroline	PB	Tri/Pres
627	Worcester Park - Wallington High School	Arriva	CN	DB250/Gem
628	Kingsbury - Southgate	Arriva	LV	DB250/ALX400
629	Wood Green Station - St. Ignatius College	Arriva	AD	DB250/Pres
				Env400
632	Kilburn Park - Grahame Park Corner Mead	Metroline	W	Tri/ALX400
				Tri/Pres
634	Muswell Hill - Barnet Hospital	Arriva	AD	DB250/Pres
				Env400

No.	Route	Operator	Garage	Type Used
635	Brentford - Sunbury St. Paul's School	Metroline	AH	Tri/Pres
636	Kemnal College - Bromley South	Stagecoach	TB	Tri/ALX400
637	Kemnal College - Bromley South	Stagecoach	TB	Tri/ALX400
638	Coney Hall - Kemnal College	Stagecoach	TB	Tri/ALX400
639	Clapham Junction - Putney Heath John Paul II School	Go-Ahead	SW	B7TL/Gem B7TL/Pres
640	South Harrow - Clamp Hill	Arriva Shires	GR	DB300/Gem2
641	West Molesey - Teddington School	Quality Line	EB	Versa Dar/ALX200
642	West Hendon - Canons Corner	Arriva Shires	GR	DB250/ALX400 Env400
643	Brent Cross - East Finchley Cemetery	Metroline	W	Tri/ALX400 Tri/Pres
646	Noak Hill - Cranham	First	DM	Dar/Cap Env200
647	Romford - Harold Hill Community School	Stagecoach	NS	Tri/ALX400
648	Romford - Cranham	First	DM	Tri/Pres
649	Romford - County Park Campion School	Go-Ahead	BE	B7TL/Pres
650	Romford - Emerson Park School	Go-Ahead	BE	B7TL/Pres
651	Romford - Chase Cross	Go-Ahead	BE	B7TL/Pres
652	Abbey Wood Lane - Upminster Station	First	DM	Tri/Pres
653	Muswell Hill - Kingsbury	Arriva	LV	DB250/ALX400
654	Addington Interchange - Ramsden Priory School	Metrobus	MB	N94/Omni
655	Mitcham - Raynes Park High School	Go-Ahead	AL	B7TL/Gem B7TL/ Pres
656	Gallows Corner - Emerson Park School	First	DM	Tri/Pres
657	Crooked Billet - Woodford Wells Bancroft's School	Arriva	EC	DB250/ALX400
658	Woolwich - Crown Woods School	Stagecoach	TL	Tri/ALX400
660	Bellingham - Crown Woods School	Stagecoach	TL	Tri/ALX400
661	Petts Wood Station - Mottingham Eltham College	Go-Ahead	BX	B7TL/Pres
664	HomEstead Way - Biggin Hill Charles Darwin School	Stagecoach	TB	Tri/ALX400
665	Surbiton - Holy Cross School	London United	TV	Dar/Point
667	Ilford - West Hatch School	Arriva	DX	B7TL/Gem DB250/ALX400
669	Thamesmead - Albany Park Cleeve Park School	Go-Ahead	BV	B7TL/Gem B7TL/Pres
670	Clapham Junction - Putney Heath John Paul II School	Go-Ahead	SW	B7TL/Gem B7TL/Pres
671	Chessington South Station - Tiffin Girls' School	London United	FW	Tri/ALX400
672	Thamesmead Woolwich Polytechnic School - Woolwich	Stagecoach	PD	Tri/ALX400
673	Warren School - Beckton	Go-Ahead	SI	B7TL/Pres
674	Dagnam Park Drive - Romford	Stagecoach	BE	B7TL/Pres
675	Walthamstow - Woodbridge High School	CT Plus	HK	Tri/Pres
678	Beckton - Stratford	Stagecoach	WH	Tri/ALX400
679	Goodmayes - Woodford Wells	First	DM	Tri/Pres
681	Hounslow - Teddington School	London United	FW	Tri/ALX400
683	Friern Barnet - Kingsbury	Arriva	LV	DB250/Pres
685	Warlingham School - Selsdon	Arriva	TC	DB250/ALX400 DB250/Gem
686	Romford Station - St. Edward's School	First	DM	Tri/Pres
687	Dagenham Park School - Barking	Stagecoach	BK	Env400
688	Southgate - Kingsbury	Arriva	LV	DB250/ALX400
690	West Norwood - Burntwood School	Arriva	N	DB250/ALX400
691	Ham Fire Station - Hollyfield School	London United	FW	Tri/ALX400
692	Potters Bar Dame Alice Owen's School - Green Dragon Lane	First	NP	Tri/Pres
696	Carnarvon Drive - Bishop Ramsey School	London United	AV	B7TL/ALX400 B7TL/Pres
697	Kinghill Avenue - Ickenham	London United	AV	B7TL/ALX400 B7TL/Pres

No.	Route	Operator	Garage	Type Used
698	West Drayton - Ickenham	London United	HH	N94/Omni
699	Green Dragon Lane - Potters Bar Dame Alice Owen's School	First	NP	Tri/Pres
H1	Golders Green - Henrietta Barnett School	Arriva	GR	Solo

900 series

No.	Route	Operator	Garage	Type Used
931	Crystal Palace - Lewisham (Fridays only)	Abellio	BC	Dar/Point Env200
941	Bedfont Green - Hampton Hill Sainsbury's (Wednesdays only)	Abellio	TF	Dar/Nimb

The 900 series, or 'mobility routes', are declining fast. Introduced to help the disabled go shopping, usually on market days, their reason to exist was undermined by the rapid introduction London-wide of low-floor buses equipped as standard with wheelchair ramps and 'squat' capability. Route 953 pictured here continues to make two return trips on Wednesdays only.

953	Scrattons Farm - Romford (Wednesdays only)	First	DM	Dar/Cap
965	Riverhill - Kingston Sainsbury's (Mondays & Fridays only)	London United	TV	Env200
969	Whitton - Roehampton Vale Asda (Fridays only)	Abellio	TF	Dar/Nimb

And For An Encore . . .

While you're out searching for the regular fleets working TfL contracts, your vision will frequently be obscured by large brown or cream objects known as London Sightseeing Tour buses. Some of you may become endlessly fascinated by this unexpected addition and search out fleet lists, while photographers will marvel at how they repeatedly block the view at the worst possible moment.

As well as the Routemasters on the two heritage routes, not a day passes without one or more privately-owned buses hoving into view. A small number work for small-scale sightseeing concerns, while the "Get Married in a Routemaster" movement is gaining ground so rapidly that one cannot move for RMs tied up with white ribbons on Saturdays. Private hire of RMs for other purposes (whatever they might be) is also common.

Aficionados of the older types will be pleased to hear that many continue in service as training vehicles and can be spotted almost anywhere from Wimbledon to Wood Green, from Hornchurch to Hounslow.

Then, there's the Commercial Services fleet operated by Go-Ahead, providing transport to and from major events in London, like the Chelsea Flower Show and Wimbledon Tennis. Although the fleet has permanent members, it is often complemented by last-minute additions from Go-Ahead garages in south London, so you never know what will turn up . . . yet more interest in the unique environment of the capital city.

Having said all that, the first two photos are almost conventional:

Stagecoach's 18500 was the first Enviro400 to arrive in London, but not the first to enter service. The bus was a replacement for the ALX400 blown up by a terrorist bomb in Tavistock Square on the 7th of July 2005. Fittingly, it continues to carry the name *Spirit of London* in its new guise of 19000.

From time to time, a small number of London's buses appear in all-over advertising livery. Go-Ahead's WVL130, working route 11 in Buckingham Palace Road, carries an advert for the Malaysian tourist board. Some of these ads last for a few months, this one lasted only a week or two.

Part of Abellio's collection of buses for disposal, currently stored at Battersea garage. The ALX400s include 9719, 9732, 9738, 9708, 9704, 9728 & 9714. The white bus is 9711, latterly operated by Abellio Surrey on the Kingston University service.

In addition to the 'heritage route' Routemasters, a number of others ply their trade for various purposes. RML2621, for instance, provides a mini sightseeing tour for Harrod's customer – hence the loss of part of its roof. Here the bus uses Thurloe Place, near South Kensington station, to turn round.

The London Necrobus, operated by Ghostbustours (geddit?) can be quite startling if it catches you unawares. RML2566 cruises Whitehall.

The Big Bus Company, as its name suggests, is one of the biggest providers of sightseeing tours in the capital. ML153, a tri-axle MCW Metrobus, takes a rest in the sunshine at Beddington.

DA205 sets off from Aldwych. This is one of twenty 10m Visionaires with Volvo B9TL chassis operated by Big Bus.

One of the more popular members of the Commercial Services fleet is this roofless Volvo Olympian/Palatine 2. The fleet turns out for a number of big events in London, like the Wimbledon tennis championships. NV171 picks up outside Wimbledon railway station during the 2011 tournament.